𝔓oems

William Sharp

Alpha Editions

This edition published in 2019

ISBN : 9789353868208

Design and Setting By
Alpha Editions
email - alphaedis@gmail.com

P O E M S

BY WILLIAM SHARP

SELECTED AND ARRANGED BY
MRS. WILLIAM SHARP

NEW YORK
DUFFIELD AND COMPANY
1912

FOREWORD

THE writings of William Sharp divide themselves in the midway of his literary life into two distinct phases. The more racially imaginative phase, put forward under shelter of a pseudonym, has been gathered together in the "Fiona Macleod" Series published by Mr. Heinemann ; and it seems fitting that a companion Series of writings of William Sharp, signed with his own name, should follow, and be as representative as possible, so that the two phases of his work can be compared conveniently.

As the " W. S." writings extend over a period of thirty years (the " F. M." period coincided with the last twelve years of the author's life), and comprise a wide range of subjects—poems, fiction, biographies, essays critical and reminiscent, and a mass of ephemeral work urged by the necessities of daily life—it has been somewhat difficult to determine on what basis to make a selection for the present Series. Finally, I decided to make choice from among the shorter poems, from essays and tales, to the exclusion of the longer novel and biography, and thus, moreover, to fulfil certain of his expressed wishes.

In the arrangement of these volumes I have not preserved a definite chronological order, except in that of songs and poems. I have preferred to group the contents according to their subjects : Vol. I. Poems : Vol. II. Critical Essays : Vols. III. and IV. Papers, Biographic and Reminiscent : Vol. V. Short Stories. With the exception of a few of the poems, early experimental work is unrepresented ; the earliest prose work included is the essay on the sonnet written in the author's thirty-first year. In accordance with his own wishes his *Life of Rossetti* —considered by him as youthful and unbalanced—also his romance, *The Children of To-morrow*, are not reissued. Of his later novels, *Wives in Exile* and *Silence Farm* (both out of print) were written during the " Fiona Macleod " period out of a desire to strengthen the reputation of " W. S." and thus help to shield the identity of " F. M." My husband considered that *Silence Farm* contained his most successful effort in characterisation. Nevertheless, in it, he deliberately suppressed certain qualities natural to him, and emphasised others in order to make the style of writing as unlike that of " Fiona Macleod " as possible. Of other excluded mature work; the monographs on Shelley, Browning, and Heine are available among the publications of Messrs. Walter Scott, to whom I am indebted for permission to include in this volume the ballads of " The Weird of Michael Scott," " The Death-Child," and " The Isle of Lost Dreams." *The Life and Letters of Joseph Severn* is out of print ; and the *Progress of Art in the XIX Century* is published by Messrs W. and R. Chambers.

The poems in the present volume (1879–1905) are selected from five volumes and a number of miscellaneous poems published in his own name, and not from those written over the pseudonym of " Fiona Macleod " (1893–1905). The earliest volume, *The Human Inheritance* (Elliot Stock, 1882) opened with a long poem in four cycles descriptive of Childhood, Youth, Manhood, and Old Age ; and from it are taken " Childhood's Inheritance," " Motherhood," &c. The sonnets " Spring Wind " and " A Midsummer Hour " were included in *The Sonnets of this Century* (Walter Scott),

as were also those " To D. G. Rossetti,"
to whose memory the anthology was dedi-
cated. *Earth's Voices* (Elliot Stock, 1884),
dedicated to Walter Pater, contained a
series of lyrics—voices of the forests, rivers,
winds, flowers, mountains, oceans—two
long poems, "Sospitra" and "Gaspara
Stampa," from which "To suffer grief is
to be strong" and "Sleep" are taken.
"The Record" is autobiographic, inasmuch
as it was the beginning of an endeavour
to relate memories of past lives that haunted
the author.

Romantic Ballads (Walter Scott, 1888)
was written under "the earnest conviction
that a Romantic Revival is imminent in our
poetic literature " ; that, as he stated in the
Preface, "the third great epoch of English
poetic literature will be an essentially
dramatic one : and its fruitage will neces-
sarily be preceded by a blossoming of the
genuinely romantic sentiment . . . of the
Romantic spirit—not the formal letter of
Romanticism—a renascence which will be
as manifest in realistic as well as in more
directly imaginative prose and poetry. . . .
In ' The Weird of Michael Scott ' [of which
two sections are herein included] I have
attempted a ballad in enlarged form—that

is, it is meant as a lyrical tragedy of a soul
that finds the face of disastrous fate against
it whithersoever it turns in the closing
moment of mortal life." And he adds, " The
thrill of the supernatural is so keen because
it touches the most natural part of us."

The poet spent the winter and spring
of 1890–91 in Rome and its environ-
ments ; the immediate literary outcome
thereof was a volume of unrhymed, irregu-
lar metres, printed at Tivoli, published
privately that spring under the title of
Sospiri di Roma and prefaced by an
etched portrait of him by Sir Charles
Holroyd. Concerning his use of unrhymed
metre he wrote to a friend : " What can be
done in Greek and German can be done in
English. This has been proved, for some
of Matthew Arnold's finest work is in
unrhymed verse. . . . I felt that there is
in verse, as in painting, a borderland for
impressionism pure and simple, for the
suggestion of a certain colour and emotion,
a vivid actuality, which are apt to be
dissipated by the effort and restrictions of
rhyme. . . . In this verse you will find
something of my passion for the Campagna,
and of that still deeper passion and longing
for the Beautiful. All that I attempt to

do is to fashion anew something of the lovely vision I have seen."

" The Coming of Love," " The Untold Story," and " Dionysos in India " appeared originally in *The Pagan Review* (1892), the first and only number of a projected monthly review edited by " W. H. Brooks "—of which William Sharp wrote every word from cover to cover, under the pseudonyms of the Editor and the seven contributors.

Of the section of poems 1893–1905, " Hill Water " was written for the *Evergreen*, 1895, a quarterly issued by Patrick Geddes and Colleagues, and " Spanish Roses " is taken from *A Fellow and His Wife*, a novel written in collaboration with Blanche Willis Howard ; the remaining poems in the last section were contributed variously to *Harper's Magazine*, the *Century*, *New York Independent*, *Literature*, *Country Life*, and the *Pall Mall Magazine*.

The Fragment entitled " Persephoneia " is the Prologue to a five-act play, begun in 1903 at Il Castello di Maniace, on Etna ; and of it the complete draft, the Prologue, and half the first act only were written.

Elizabeth A. Sharp

CONTENTS

xi

Contents

Contents

Contents

xiv

Contents

FROM

THE HUMAN
INHERITANCE

1882

Praise be the fathomless universe
For life and joy . . . and love,
sweet love.

FIRST WORDS

(To the one who has always first read everything I have written.)

How can I tell thee, dear, what never words
Have fitly told ?   How ope my heart to thee
Wherein thou mightst, as in a well, per-
    ceive
Deep down but the mere shadow of my love ?
But as the wind sweeps from the icy north
To some lov'd isle in dim Pacific seas,
Or as the never-ceasing circling waves
Follow round earth the radiant orb of night,
So follow I with love unspeakable
The pathways fill'd with light which are thine
    own.
O love, thou art the flame that burns for me,
My steady purpose !   That no dark can
    quench !
Holding thy hand I fear no more to watch
The shifting of the changeful lights of Fate.

CHILDHOOD'S INHERITANCE

I

Beneath the blue vault of a summer sky,
Where little clouds with white wings strove
    to fly
Far from the burning noon, leagues long
    there lay
Wide heather moors that stretched till far
    away
Northward faint hills arose, and southward
    rolled
The ocean gleaming with sun-litten gold.

II

And 'mid a great swell of the purple waste
Close to the sea, a rock, which no hand
    placed
Thus lonely and afar but which was hurled
A meteor from some ruin'd starry world,
Rose dark and frowning, with its hoar sides
    scarred
By winter tempests and the fiercely hard

4

Gripe of the death-frosts that from north-
    land heights
Steal silent through grim January nights,
And traced with furrows by the many tears
Of rainy autumns thro' unnumber'd years.

III

The purple moorland waste alone stretched
    wide
Beneath the sun—no thing was seen beside
To break the long still sweep that met the sky,
No mounds of rocks confusedly piled high,
No single tree with clear boughs limned in
    black
Against the blue, no white and dusty track,
But only miles and miles and miles that swept
Purple to where the leagueless waters leapt.
The old rock stood forth like an ancient throne
Great tho' forgotten, where the winds alone
Paid homage, fair in the sunshine of the day,
Solemn by night with phosphorescent grey.

IV

Around, the honey-laden bees humm'd loud
With summer gladness ; in a mazy cloud
Whirling the grey gnats rose and wheeled
    and spun
Swift golden notes within the golden sun ;

And bright with all their royal emblazonries
Flashed like swift darts of fire great dragon-
    flies.
Away across the glowing moors there rang
The lapwing's wild complaint, and far off
    sang
Hidden in blue a small rejoicing lark
Singing against some unseen yearn'd for
    mark :
About the heath the yellowhammer's cry
Piped sweet and clear, and often suddenly,
With joyous chirps and jerks, the stonechat
    flew
From spray to spray, and, darting flame-like
    through
The scented heather spires to where beneath
The ants had silent kingdoms in the heath,
The green-grey black-eyed lizard flashing shot
So swift the hawk on poised wings saw it not.

V

O'er all the deep skies arch'd a wondrous
    space
Of ardent azure while the sun had place,
That changed to dark, deep depths when
    twilight grey
Dreamt into night dark'ning to one vast
    shade.

6

Of purple-black, when lamplike star by star
Sparkled or shone or pulsing flamed afar.
Silence, save for each blent and natural
    sound
Of earth and air—where sea-caves made the
    ground,
By tidal waves of ages undermined,
Groan as in travail—when the trumpet wind
All uncheck'd blew—or swelled the incessant
    cries
Of tossed waves in their breaking agonies.

VI

Upon the summit of the ancient stone
(Whose birth was in Time's youth), and all
    alone,
Sat silent, tranced, and motionless a child,
Like some sweet flow'r chance nurtured in
    the wild,
Sat watching seabirds, with his eager eyes
Full of the deep blue of the vaulted skies.
A child, for he indeed was little more ;
A child at heart, such as whom make the
    door
Of heaven seem open'd here—to whom the
    seas
Breaking in foam, and scattered spray-swept
    trees

With long arms wrestling, and the winds on
    wings
Invisible were wondrous living things.

VII

A flower, for his wind-kissed locks unshorn
Shone yellow as gold daffodils at morn ;
His eyes were blue as in the golden grain
Windflow'rs are blue, and soft as after rain
Violets that under dripping leaves have lain,
And tender as a dappled fawn's that yearn
For pity when the shrew-mice from the fern
Shake down the dew-drops; 'neath his sunlit
    hair
As early morning, his sweet face was fair
Beneath the sun-brown—as a white bud rose
That flushes faintly while the June sun
    glows.
And even as he gazed there deeper grew
Within his eyes a holier softer blue,
Where some thought brooded in their sacred
    shade ;
It seemed almost as if some song were laid
Asleep upon his face that yet would find
Some perfect utterance for the echoing wind
To carry to the birds ; in reverie
Raptured he saw what these could never
    see.

VIII

Oh blessed time, when all God's world is fair
And to the soul not foreign ! When the bare
Wide cruel wastes of death-encumber'd sea
Seem as the voice of God that thunderingly
Beats round the recreant earth ; when
    morning seems
The revelation of one's utmost dreams
Of beauty ; when the slow death of the day
Makes all the west one glorious crimson way
For happy souls that die ; and when the
    moon,
Wheeling her radiant orb thro' the dark
    noon
Of night, with conscious splendour makes the
    seas
Unutterably solemn, and great trees
Lost in the shadow stand forth with huge
    limbs
Ghostly and clear ; when bird-songs are all
    hymns
Of joy and praise, and every wilding flower
Is known and loved ; and when each pent-
    up hour
Seems worse than wasted to the eager
    heart,
That fain would hear the thrush-wings strike
    apart

9

The beech leaves in short flight ere full and
    clear
Burst the sweet tide of song, or watch the
    deer
Stand with great eyes amid the fern, or
    high
Hearken the cuckoo's music fill the sky.

IX

He seemed content just silently to sit
And watch the breaking waves, the swallows
    flit
Like arrows through the air, save when along
The summer wind swept bearing the sweet
    song
Of happy larks, or the repeated cries
Of plovers when they caught the hawk's
    keen eyes
Fixt on their young—and then he seem'd to be
All sight and ear, as yearning tearfully
To beat with spirit pinions that fine air
Where at the gates of heaven exceeding fair
The bird-songs rose and fell like silver tides,
Or else to be as that royal bird that prides
Itself on flinching not before the sun
But stares undaunted, so he might have spun
Downward with death upon the fierce pois'd
    hawk,

Saving the moorland brood : not man or boy
Seem'd he so much as some incarnate joy
At one with all things fair, flow'r o' the sod
And insect, to the Loveliness call'd God.

X

As a red rose that in full bloom doth spread
Her soft flushed bosom to the wind ere dead
'Mid fallen leaves her queenliness is gone,
So the fair westering day in glory shone
Heedless of coming night though night was
    nigh.
The sunset burned afar ; the holy sky
Seem'd filled with heavenly forms mail'd in
    clear gold,
Guiding their purple rafts through seas that
    rolled
Immeasurably far off in crimson fire.
The sea lay tranced watching the day expire,
And tired waves rose and fell as though each
    pray'r
Of rest long sought were granted. Every-
    where
God's blessing brooded. And at last the day
With one long earthward smile, dissolved away,
Veiling her head in twilight robes where-
    through
The palpitating stars shone faint and few.

XI

From out the darkening vault where they
    had hid
Through sweltering heats of noon, swiftly
    there slid
Star after star, each swimming from the near
Dark blue of heaven, as from a windless mere
Rise in calm morning twilights white and
    clear
Young lily buds that open golden eyes
Which joy makes wider when the day doth
    rise.

XII

Far inland, with an oft-repeated cry
The curlew wailed, and swelled mysteriously
Hoarse sounds from the dim sea. The boy's
    face grew
White in the dusky shade as swiftly flew
A great grey gull close by him, like a ghost
Haunting the desolate margins of the
    coast :
Great moths came out, with myriad sharded
    wings
Huge beetles droned, and other twilight
    things
Hummed their dim lives away, and through
    the air

Childhood's Inheritance

The flittermice wheeled whistling : while the
    glare
Of summer lightnings flashing furtively
Blazed for a moment o'er the sleeping sea.

XIII

At last, with a long sigh, he turn'd and slid
From the old rock, and for a little hid
His face amongst the heather-spires that
    shook
With cool sweet dews : then one last
    lingering look
Across the twilight seas, whereo'er the moon
Within her crescent shallop would sail soon,
When with swift steps he turn'd and west-
    ward fled
Across the moor by a little path that led,
Almost unseen save known, till suddenly,
Screened from the vision of the neighbouring
    sea
Low in a dip between two moorland mounds
A cottage lay ; whereto with rapid bounds
He sped, and, bearing with him odours of
    salt foam,
Entered the little doorway of his home.

YOUNG LOVE

On a flower in a forest,
　A lily-bosom'd flower,
(Where never windy tempest
　Came, nor ever any shower)—
A golden hour of birthtide,
　(The sky was blue, so blue !)
Left me lying 'mid a songtide
　Of birds of every hue.

Upon the white flower swaying
　I laughed and sang in glee,
Till the thrushes long delaying
　Sang back deliciously ;
And the dear white cloudlets sleeping
　Up in the blue, blue sky,
Seem'd downy cherubs peeping
　Between the pine boughs high.

A little wind came blowing
　And sang a wild-wood song,
It whispered of the flowing
　Of bubbling streams along ;
I laughed, and stood, and rising
　Found I had two small wings—
So then I flew rejoicing
　Toward the water-springs.

Young Love

And ever 'mid my flying,
  (A little cloud I seem'd !)
I heard a great deep sighing,
  As earth in trouble dream'd ;
And when I reached the river
  The sound more windlike blew :
The glad stream lisped " for ever,"
  But the sighing grew and grew.

And as I laughed and wonder'd
  Among the flowers and grass,
All suddenly it thunder'd,
  The sunlight seem'd to pass :
A great wind took and blew me
  Across a grey wet sand,
And tho' I wept it threw me
  Far from the joyous land.

And now the salt waves leaping
  Pursue with hungry springs,
And baffled, blind, and weeping,
  I beat my draggled wings :
This was the great deep sighing
  I heard when I was young—
And now, wind-weary, dying,
  My last sob-note is sung !

MOTHERHOOD

Beneath the awful full-orb'd moon
 The silent tracts of wild-rice lay
Dumb since the fervid heat of noon
 Beat through the burning Indian day ;
And still as some far tropic sea
Where no winds murmur, no waves be.

The bending seeded tops alone
 Swayed in the sleepy sultry wind,
Which came and went with frequent moan
 As though some dying place to find ;
While at sharp intervals there rang
The fierce cicala's piercing clang.

Deep 'mid the rice-field's green-hued gloom
 A tigress lay with birth-throes ta'en ;
Her serpent tail swept o'er her womb
 As if to sweep away the pain
That clutched her by the gold-barred thighs
And shook her throat with snarling cries.

Her white teeth tore the wild-rice stems ;
 And as she moaned her green eyes grew
Lurid like shining baleful gems
 With fires volcanic lighten'd through,

While froth fell from her churning jaws
Upon her skin-drawn gleaming claws.

As in a dream at some strange sound
    The soul doth seem to freeze, so she
Lay fixed like marble on the ground,
    Changed in a moment : suddenly,
A far-off roar of savage might
Boomed through the silent sultry night.

Her eyes grew large and flamed with fire ;
    Her body seem'd to feel the sound
And thrill therewith, as thrills a lyre
    When wild wind wakes it with a bound
And sweeps its string-clasp'd soul along
In waves of melancholy song.

Her answering howl swept back again
    And eddied to her far mate's ear ;
Then once again the travail-pain
    Beat at the heart that knew no fear,
But some new instinct seem'd to rise
And yearn and wonder in her eyes.

Did presage of the coming birth
    Light up her life with mother-love,
As winds along the morning earth
    Whisper of golden dawn above ?
Or was it but some sweet wild thought
Remember'd vaguely ere forgot ?

Motherhood

Some sweet wild thought of that still night
 When underneath the low-lying moon,
Vast, awful, in its splendour white,
 Two tigers fought for love's last boon :
Two striped and fire-eyed terrors strove
Through blood and foam to reach her love.

Of how their fight so deathly still
 Fill'd all her heart with savage glee ;
The lust to love, to slay, to kill,—
 The fierce desire with him to be
Whose fangs all bloody from the fray
Should turn triumphantly away :

Of how at last with one wild cry
 One gript the other's throat and breath,
And, with hell gleaming thro' each eye,
 Shook the wild life to loveless death ;
Then stood with waving tail and ire
Triumphant changed to swift desire ?

But once again the bitter strife
 Of wrestling sinews shook her there ;
And soon a little mewling life
 Met her bewilder'd yearning stare,
Till, through her pain, the tigress strove
With licking tongue her love to prove.

No longer fearless flamed the light
 Of great green eyes straight thro' the
  gloom,

Motherhood

Each nerve seem'd laden with affright,
　The eyes expectant of some doom ;
The very moonlight's steady glare
Beat hungrily about her lair.

A beetle rose, and hummed, and hung
A moment ere it fled—but great
In face of peril to her young
　The tigress rose supreme in hate
And, with tail switching and lips drawn,
The unreal foe scowled out upon.

And when a mighty cobra, coiled
　Amid the tangled grass-roots near,
Hissed out his hunger, her blood boiled
　With rage that left no room for fear,
Till, with a howl that shook the dark,
She sprang and left him cold and stark.

But when a feeble hungry wail
　Smote on her yearning ears she turn'd
With velvet paws and refluent tail
　And eyes that no more flashed and burn'd
But flamed throughout the solemn night
Like lamps of soft sweet yellow light

To where her young was ; where she lay
　Silent, and full of some strange love
Long hours.　Along the star-strewn way
　A comet flashed and flamed above,

19

And where great wastes of solemn blue
Spread starless sailed the vast moon through,
No sound disturb'd the tigress, save
  Stray jackals, or some wild boar's pant
Where thickest did the tall rice wave,
  Or trump of distant elephant ;
Or, when these fill'd the night no more,
The tiger's deep tremendous roar.

II

Vast, solitary, gloomful, dark,
  Primeval forests swept away
To where the gum and stringy bark
  Against great granite mountains lay ;
And through their depths the twilight stole
And dusk'd still deeper each dark bole.

Deep in their pathless tracks there reared
  A huge white gum, whose giant height
When winds infrequent blew appeared
  To brush the stars out from the night :
A mighty column, straight and vast,
Solemn with immemorial past :

And at its base upon a bed
  Of fern-tree leaves strewn o'er the ground
A woman lay as though lying dead—
  Dark, rigid still, without one sound :
Her fixed eyes lifted not, nor saw
The great stars tremble in strange awe.

Motherhood

Crouch'd near upon the tufted grass
  Two wither'd, long-haired women bent
Two dusky bodies. No sign was
  Made ever them between, nor went
From swift, slant, startled eyes a glance
To break the spell of their deep trance.

They crouch'd with heads bent down
      between
  Thin, black uprisen knees ; their hair
Hid their dark faces like a screen,
  And, scored with thorns, their feet lay
      bare :
Hour after hour had watched them so,
Three shadows fixt in sphinx-like woe.

At times some wandering parrot's voice
  Clanged through the dusk ; from dead
      trees nigh
A locust whirred its deafening noise
  And shrilled th' opossum's frequent cry :
And hour by hour some slim snake stole
Hissing from fallen rotting bole.

At last, above the farthest range
  The full vast moon sail'd o'er the trees :
The dead-like woman felt some change
  Thrill thro' her body ; from her knees
Each shadow-watcher raised her head,
And stared with eyes of moveless dread.

Motherhood

Beyond—within the ghastly shade
    Of time-forgotten-gums aglow
With phosphorescent light that made
    Each trunk burn taper-like—bent low,
A savage, bearded and long-haired,
Wild-eyed across the pale gloom stared :

And when his shifting, restless eyes
    Caught the drawn woman's birthtime
        pang,
He shrilled a wild yell to the skies
    And high with tossing arms upsprang
Beating with eager blows a drum
And shivering with some terror dumb :

The list'ning women once again
    Shudder'd and grew more chill with
        fear—
Not at the harsh drum's maddening strain
    But at the spirits that were near,
The awful souls of hated dead
That creep round each wild travail-bed ;

The white-eyed sheeted things that steal
    Down dusky ways, and lie in wait
And from the shade their death-darts wheel
    And wreak unseen their deathless hate :
For these the fierce drum clanged and beat
The summons of a swift retreat.

22

Motherhood

What strange thoughts wander'd thro' the
    mind
  Of her who writhed in travail sore ?
As, bearing scents and sounds, a wind
  Blows pregnant from some distant shore,
So may have blown some wind of thought
Memorious from a past forgot,

Drifting across her yearning eyes
  Stray visions of lost happy days,
And filling with strange vague surprise
  The dreary sameness of her gaze—
Dim, sweet memorial hours long lost,
Scorched by long suns, numbed by long frost.

But soon the wafted breaths that blew
  From off the deep drown'd past were
    blown
Aside before some sharp wind new
  Of sudden agony. A moan
Shook on her lips, and from her womb
A new life crept to outer gloom.

The watching women rose and went
  With deft hands unto her : the man
Hush'd his tempestuous instrument,
  And with fleet silent footsteps ran
To where, asleep in moonlight, lay
Some huts rough built from branches stray :

Motherhood

And soon thereafter, in the light
  Of the full moon, the tribe stole out
And fill'd with cries the startled night—
  Till, with claspt hands and one wild shout,
They circled round the riven frame
Of her whose blank eyes knew no shame.

But as some feeble strength came back
  She stretched out thin and claw-like hands,
With eyes as one who on a rack
  Yearns for mercy, or on strange lands
Lifts outspread arms towards his own—
So yearn'd she, with a mother's moan.

Within her famish'd eyes no more
  The hunger of the body burned,
But on the fruit her womb long bore
  Their light unspeakable was turned :
And all the hunger of her love
Lighten'd the child's eyes from above.

Vast, solitary, gloomful, dark,
  Primeval forests swept away
To where the gum and stringy bark
  Against the granite mountains lay :
Till, as the great moon grew more wan,
Stirred the first heart-beats of the dawn.

And o'er the pathless tracks where reared
  The huge white gum, whose boughs had
    seen

Motherhood

The woman's birth-throes, light appeared
   And lit its leaves with golden green,
And shone upon the straight trunk vast,
Solemn with immemorial past.

III

Faint scent of lilies filled the room,
   Hush'd in sweet silence and asleep
Within the dim delicious gloom :
   No windy lamp-flame strove to leap
Amidst the moveless shade, but faint
A soft light burned from censer quaint.

And dimly through the gloom loomed large
   A carven bed that seem'd to sail
Like ghost of some great funeral barge
   'Mid shadow-seas no men might hail—
Till from its depths suffused with night
The wan sheets dreamed to gleaming white.

And lo, half-hid, like some white flow'r
   Breasting the driven snow, there lay
Expectant of the awful hour
   A waiting girl, who, far away
Beyond where vision reacheth, gazed
With eyes by some strange glory dazed.

Motherhood

Like two strange dreams they were, wherein
    Played subtle lights of other life,
Deep depths, scarce cognisant of sin,
    Serene, beyond all clamorous strife—
Two seas unsoundable as night
Yet lit to utmost depths with light.

Silent she lay, as one who low
    In some dim vast deserted nave
Bends rapt in mingled love and woe
    While the wild, passionate, sweeping wave
Of organ music sweeps and rolls—
The burden of all suffering souls.

Silent she lay, for as a palm
    Within a thirsty desert feels
A low wind break the deathly calm
    And drinks each rain-drop as it steals
Between its dry parch'd leaves, so she
Felt God's breath fill her fitfully.

The soft low wind of life divine
    Entered the darkened womb, and there
It cleft the mystic bands that twine
    The folded bud of childhood fair,
Which, as an open'd lily, fell
From death to life's strange miracle.

26

Motherhood

O perfect bud of human flow'r
   Immaculately sweet and pure,
Shall God's first influence in this hour
   Through all thy coming life endure,
And thou expand to perfect bloom
Untouched by crash of neighbouring doom ?

Or, O sweet perfect human bud,
   Shall rains thee dash, and wild winds sweep
Thy fair head to the mire and mud,
   And, with praying hands, thy mother weep
Such tears of anguish as no pain
Shall ever wring from her again ?

Soft, soft, the wind of life doth breathe :—
   Some angel surely fans the while
The faint new-litten spark beneath,
   And prayeth with a piteous smile
That it may live, and living be
A victor 'midst humanity.

Silent she lay who soon should give
   This life to life : her secret thought
Strove 'mid the happy past to live
   Again that day she ne'er forgot,
That day when her young love took wing
From maidenhood's sweet-scented spring :

Motherhood

When hand in hand she trod the ways
  Flow'r-strewn with him, and felt his eyes
Turn'd full on her with such deep gaze
  Of love triumphant, that the skies
Seem'd but a hollow dome where rang
Sweet tumult, as though angels sang :

How the hush'd drowsy afternoon
  Slipt through the summertide, till low
In the dark tranquil east the moon
  Rose vast and yellow, and more slow
The flaming star that lights the west
Lulled the sea-waters to their rest :

How in the bridal chamber shone
  No other than the full-moon's light,
And how between the dusk and dawn
  A wind of passion fill'd the night
And bore resistless soul with soul
On to love's utmost crowning goal.

Silent she was, but as her mind
  Made real once more that perfect day
Her body trembled, as a wind
  Had blown upon her where she lay,
And in her eyes serene and deep
Joys unforgotten woke from sleep.

28

Motherhood

As on a mighty midnight sea
    Wind-swept, and lit by a white glare
Where intermittent lightnings flee
    And deafened by the thunderous air
Split up with tumult, one great wave
Doth rise and scorn an ocean-grave,

And, gathering volume as it rolls,
    Doth sweep triumphant till at last
It thunders up the sounding shoals
    Of stricken promontory aghast,
And leaves its crown of foam where high
The cliffs stare seaward steadily :

So from love's throbbing pulsing sea
    All lightning-lit by passion, reared
A mighty wave resistlessly
    Of mother-love, which as it neared
Fulfilment broke in one glad cry
Of sweet half-wond'ring ecstasy.

Hush ! the great sea is still, and low
    The night-wind wanders ; hush, for calm
The mother waits the body's woe.
    Silent she lay ; mayhap a psalm
Of sacred joy sang deep within
The maiden heart unstained by sin.

Motherhood

Mayhap the inward vision saw
   The unborn soul arise and stand
Great in a people's love and awe,
   Crown'd not with gold by human hand
But sacred with the bays that wait
The victor in the strife of Fate :

And deeper still, beheld afar
   The billows of the ages sweep
A mightier soul from star to star—
   So ever upwards through the steep
Dim ways of God's unfathom'd will
But aye by fuller periods still.

So shall it be for ever : evermore
The mystic wheel of mother-love shall whirl
Around the world, and link these three again.

THE REDEEMER

I know that my Redeemer liveth—but out
    of the depths of time
He hath not called to me yet. But from th'
    immeasurable tracts
That widen unending to where beginneth
    eternity
Falleth at times a voice, heart-thrilling,
    soul-piercing, life-giving ;
High sometimes and clear, as a lark singing
    in a holy dawn,
Hush'd and afar off again as a dreaming
    wave upon seas
Lit by a low vast moon, and windlessly
    sleeping, but ever
Sweet with a human love, and full of
    ineffable yearning,
And crying of soul unto soul from infinite
    deep unto deep.
And sometimes I look and gaze out upon
    uttermost darkness
And hear the wail of desolate winds moaning
    around the world—

The Redeemer

Till the darkness shivers to light, and
    clashing thro' earth and heaven
I hear great wings make music, and mar-
    vellous thunderous songs
Shout " Thy Redeemer liveth, O human
    soul, and crieth for thee ! "

LINES TO E. A. S.

Fair in my sight as white lilies that shine in
    the sunrise :
Sweeter than flow'rs in the meadows that
    scent the mornings of spring :
Dearer than vision of truth, for thou art the
    truth revealèd,
Dearer than faith, for thou art the crown
    of aspiration,
Dearer than hope, for of hope thou art the
    fulfilment !
O love, love, love, thou hast turned the
    darkness of the world
Into ineffable light, and all its intricate
    ways
To straight, clear paths that lead from the
    depths to the heavens.
The flower of my soul sways high in the wind
    of thy love,
Glowing with passionate fervour through
    fulness of joy ;
Soul with soul are we wedded, beyond the
    decay of the body,

Lines to E. A. S.

And spirit hath spirit touched, beyond the
    confines of flesh :
Desire with mighty wings hath swept the
    chords of our being,
And flesh and spirit are one in the mystic
    union of love !

SONNETS
1882–1886

SPRING WIND

O full-voiced herald of immaculate Spring,
  With clarion gladness striking every tree
  To answering raptures, as a resonant sea
Fills rock-bound shores with thunders echo-
    ing—
O thou, each beat of whose tempestuous
    wing
  Shakes the long winter-sleep from hill and
    lea,
  And rouses with loud reckless jubilant glee
The birds that have not dared as yet to
    sing :

O Wind that comest with prophetic cries,
  Hast thou indeed beheld the face that is
  The joy of poets and the glory of birds—
Spring's face itself : hast thou 'neath bluer
    skies
  Met the warm lips that are the gates of
    bliss,
  And heard June's leaf-like murmur of
    sweet words ?

A MIDSUMMER HOUR

There comes not through the o'erarching
    cloud of green
A harsh, an envious sound to jar the ear :
But vaguely swells a hum, now far, now
    near,
Where the wild honey-bee beyond the
    screen
Of beech-leaves haunts the field of flowering
    bean.
Far, far away the low voice of the weir
Dies into silence. Hush'd now is the clear
Sweet song down-circling from the lark
    unseen.

Beyond me, where I lie, the shrew-mice run
    A-patter where of late the streamlet's tones
    Made music : on a branch a drowsy bird
Sways by the webs that midst dry pools are
      spun—
    Yet lives the streamlet still, for o'er flat
      stones
      The slow lapse of the gradual wave is
      heard.

PAIN

I am God's eldest :—I and Love are twin ;
  We look for ever in the other's face ;
  Together our flight wings throughout all
    space—
Sun, Star, Man, God, alike we dwell therein ;
Some far-off goal together strive to win.
  But here on earth I leave the mightier
    trace,
  Clasp hands more close with all the
    human race,
And weave the shadow-webs of joy and sin.

And most I dwell in the clear skies at dawn,
  In marvellous eves when all the stars are
    bright,
In music ere the sweetest chord is gone,
  In woman's beauty still unsoiled and
    white,
In children's slumber in the morning wan;
  And lovers' vows and yearnings in the
    night.

POSSIBILITIES

As day doth live beyond the sunset skies
  So life may wait us at the silent grave :
  Not windless is the sea because there rave
Not always the great storm-wind's har-
    monies.
There may be light too strong for earthly
    eyes ;
  There may be hands to succour and to
    save
  From Death's indifferent o'erwhelming
    wave ;
Nay, Death may lift to some divine sur-
    prise !

There may be music beyond instruments,
  And Spring for ev'ry frost-nipt shapeless
    clod,
There may be mightier love sacraments
  Than e'er were seen on consecrated sod ;
A man there may be with Christ's linea-
    ments
  And 'mid the wheels of Fate a living God.

TO D. G. ROSSETTI

I

From out the darkness cometh never a sound:
  No voice doth reach us from the silent
    place :
  There is one goal beyond life's blindfold
    race,
For victor and for victim—burial-ground.
O friend, revered, belov'd, mayst thou have
  found
  Beyond the shadowy gates a yearning face,
  A beckoning hand to guide thee with
    swift pace
From the dull wave Lethean gliding round.

Hope dwelt with thee, not Fear ; Faith;
  not Despair :
  But little heed thou hadst of the grave's
    gloom.
What though thy body lies so deeply there
  Where the land throbs with tidal surge
    and boom,
Thy soul doth breathe some Paradisal air
  And Rest long sought thou hast where
    amaranths bloom.

TO D. G. ROSSETTI

II

Yet even if Death indeed with pitiful sign
  Bade us drink deep of some oblivious
    draught,
  Is it not well to know, ere we have
    quaffed
The soul-deceiving poppied anodyne,
That not in vain erewhile we drink the
    wine
  Of life—that not all blankly or in craft
  Of evil went the days wherein we laughed
And joyed i' the sun unknowing aught
    divine ?

Not so thy doom whatever fate betide :
  Not so for thee O poet-heart and true
  Who fearless watched, as evermore it
    grew,
The shadow of Death creep closer to thy
    side.
  A glory with thy ebbing life withdrew
And we inherit now its deathless Pride.

FROM

EARTH'S VOICES

1884

MADONNA NATURA

I love and worship thee in that thy ways
Are fair, and that the glory of past days
  Haloes thy brightness with a sacred hue.
Within thine eyes are dreams of mystic
    things,
Within thy voice a subtler music rings
  Than ever mortal from the keen reeds
    drew ;
Thou weav'st a web which men have callèd
    Death
But Life is in the magic of thy breath.

The secret things of Earth thou knowest
    well ;
Thou seest the wild bee build his narrow cell,
  The lonely eagle wing through lonely skies,
The lion on the desert roam afar,
The glow-worm glitter like a fallen star,
  The hour-lived insect as it hums and flies ;
Thou seest men like shadows come and go,
And all their endless dreams drift to and
    fro.

Madonna Natura

In thee is strength, endurance, wisdom,
    truth :
Thou art above all mortal joy and ruth,
    Thou hast the calm and silence of the
    night :
Mayhap thou seest what we cannot see,
Surely far off thou hear'st harmoniously
    Echoes of flawless music infinite,
Mayhap thou feelest thrilling through each
    sod
Beneath thy feet the very breath of God.

Monna Natura, fair and grand and great,
I worship thee, who art inviolate :
    Through thee I reach to things beyond
    this span
Of mine own puny life, through thee I learn
Courage and hope, and dimly can discern
    The ever noble grades awaiting man :
Madonna, unto thee I bend and pray—
Saviour, Redeemer thou, whom none can
    slay !

No human fanes are dedicate to thee,
But thine the temples of each tameless sea,
    Each mountain-height and forest-glade
    and plain :
No priests with daily hymns thy praises
    sing,

But far and wide the wild winds chanting
    swing,
And dirge the sea-waves on the changeless
    main,
While songs of birds fill all the fields and
    woods,
And cries of beasts the savage solitudes.

Hearken, Madonna, hearken to my cry ;
Teach me through metaphors of liberty,
    Till strong and fearing nought in life or
      death
I feel thy sacred freedom through me thrill,
Wise, and defiant, with unquenchèd will
    Unyielding, though succumb the mortal
      breath—
Then if I conquer, take me by the hand
And guide me onward to thy Promised
    Land !

DURING MUSIC

O tears that well up to my eyes,
  And vague thoughts wandering thro' my
    brain,
Whence come ye ? From what alien skies,
  From what dim sorrow, what strange
    pain ?

I hear old memories astir
  In dusky twilights of the past :
O voices telling me of her,
  My soul, whom now I know at last :

I know her not by any name,
  But she with hope or fear is pale ;
I see her ere this body came
  From mortal womb with mortal wail.

Later and later through long years,
  Through generations of dead men,
I see her in her mist of tears,
  I see her in her shroud of pain.

I see her whom the æons have raised
  From one dim birth to endless life ;
I see her strive, regain, re-fail
  Forever in the endless strife.

During Music

I see her, soul of man, and soul
  Of woman, and in many lands :
Her eyes are fixt on some far goal
  But she hath neither thrall nor bands.

On one day yet to come I see
  This body pale and cold and dead :
The spirit once again made free
  Hovers triumphant overhead.

Again, again, O endless day,
  I see her in new forms pace on,
And ever with her on the way
  Fair kindred souls in unison.

O wandering thoughts within my brain,
  O voices speaking low to me,
O music sweet with stingless pain,
  Bring clear the vision that I see !

O ecstasy of sound, O pain !
  Too sad my heart, too sad the tears
It bringeth to my eyes again,
  Too strange the hopes, too strange the
    fears.

SHADOWED SOULS

If the soul withdraweth from the body, what profit
thereafter hath a man of all the days of his life ?

She died indeed, but to him her breath
Was more than a light blown out by death :
He knew that they breathed the self-same
    air,
That not midst the dead was her pale face
    fair
But that she waited for him somewhere.

To some dead city, or ancient town,
Where the mould'ring towers were crumbling
    down,
Or in some old mansion habited
By dust and silence and things long dead,
He knew the Shadows of Souls were led.

For years he wandered a weary way,
His eyes shone sadder, his hair grew grey :
But still he knew that she lived for whom
No grave lay waiting, no white carv'd tomb,
No earthly silence, no voiceless gloom.

Shadowed Souls

But once in a bitter year he came
To an old dying town with a long dead
    name :
That eve, as he walked thro' the dusty ways
And the echoes woke in the empty place,
He came on a Shadow face to face.

It looked, but uttered no word at all
Then beckoned him into an old dim hall :
And lo, as soon as he passed between
The pillars with age and damp mould green
His eyes were dazed by a strange wild
    scene.

A thousand lamps fill'd the place with light,
And fountains glimmered faerily bright ;
But never a single sound was heard,
The dreadful silence was never stirred,
Not even the breath of a single word

Came from the shadowy multitude,
More dense than leaves in a summer wood,
Than the sands where the swift tides ebb
    and flow ;
But ever the Shades moved to and fro
As windless waves on the sea will go.

Then he who had come to the Shadow-land
Swift strode by many a group and band ;

Shadowed Souls

But never a glimpse he caught of her,
In fleeting shadow or loiterer,
For whom the earth held no sepulchre.

He knew that she was not dead whom he
So loved with bitterest memory,
To whom through anguish'd years he had
    prayed ;
Yet came she never, no sign was made,
No touch on his haggard frame was laid.

At last to an empty room he came,
And there he saw in letters of flame :
" This is a palace no king controls,
A place unwritten in human scrolls,—
This is the Haunt of Shadowed Souls :

" If thy Shadow-soul be here no more,
Seek thine old life's deserted shore :
And there, mayhap, thou wilt find again,
Recovered now through sorrow and pain,
The Soul thou didst thy most to have slain."

SONG

" To suffer grief is to be strong,
 And to be strong is beautiful and rare "—
 'Twas in thy court, O Love, I learned it
   there,
  This sad sweet song !

No one man dwells thy ways among,
 Who shall not learn thy thousand ways
   of grief
 Or how wild fears succeed each poor
  relief
  In dark'ning throng :

There too a man may learn to put away
 The crownèd summit of his heart's
   desire ;
 But O, the bitter burning of love's fire—
  Its bitterer ashes grey !

SLEEP

While sways the restless sea
  Beyond the shore,
And the waves sing listlessly
  Their secret lore,
And the soft fragrant air
  From off the deep
Scarce stirs thine outspread hair,—
    Sleep !

Far up in purple skies
  Great lamps hang out,
White flames that fall and rise
  In motley rout ;
While fall their silvern rays
  O'er crag and steep,
Woodlands and meadow-ways,—
    Sleep !

While the moon's amber gleams
  Gild rock and flow'r,
Let no untimely dreams
  Possess the hour :
Let no vague fears the heart
  'Mid slumber keep,
In dreams love hath no smart,—
    Sleep !

MATER DOLOROSA

She, brooding ever, dwells amidst the hills ;
  Her kingdom is call'd Solitude ; her
      name—
  More terrible than desolating flame—
  Is Silence ; and her soul is Pain.
Day after day some weightier sorrow fills
  Her heart, and each new hour she knows
    The birth of further woes.
    And whoso, journeying, goes
Unto the land wherein she dwells for aye
Shall not come thence until have passed
      away
  For evermore the bright joy of his years.
  She giveth rest, but giveth it with tears,
    Tears that more bitter be
    Than drops of the Dead Sea :
But never gives she peace to any soul
  For how could she that rarest gift bestow
    Who well doth know
That though in dreams she can attain the
      goal,
  In dreams alone her steps can thither
      go :—

55

Mater Dolorosa

Solitude, Silence, Pain, for all who live
  Within the twilit realms that are her own,
  And even Rest to those who seek her
    throne,
    But these her gifts alone :
Peace hath she not and therefore cannot
    give.

THE SONG OF THE THRUSH

When the beech-trees are green in the
    woodlands,
  And the thorns are whitened with may,
And the meadow-sweet blows and the
    yellow gorse blooms
    I sit on a wind-waved spray,
    And I sing through the livelong day
  From the golden dawn till the sunset
    comes and the shadows of gloaming
    grey.

And I sing of the joy of the woodlands,
  And the fragrance of wild-wood flowers,
And the song of the trees and the hum of
    the bees
    In the honeysuckle bowers,
    And the rustle of showers
  And the voice of the west wind calling as
    through glades and green branches he
    scours.

When the sunset glows over the woodlands
  More sweet rings my lyrical cry,

The Song of the Thrush

With the pain of my yearning to be 'mid
    the burning
  And beautiful colours that lie
  'Midst the gold of the sun-down sky,
Where over the purple and crimson and
  amber the rose-pink cloud-curls fly.

Sweet, sweet swells my voice thro' the
    woodlands,
  Repetitive, marvellous, rare :
And the song-birds cease singing as my
    music goes ringing
  And eddying echoing there,
  Now wild and now debonair,
Now fill'd with a tumult of passion that
  throbs like a pulse in the hush'd warm
  air !

THE SONG OF FLOWERS

What is a bird but a living flower ?
A flower but the soul of some dead bird ?
And what is a weed but the dying breath
Of a perjured word ?

A flower is the soul of a singing-bird,
Its scent is the breath of an old-time song :
But a weed and a thorn spring forth each
    day
For a new-done wrong.

Dead souls of song-birds, thro' the green
    grass,
Or deep in the midst of the golden grain,
In woodland valley, where hill-streams pass,
We flourish again.

We flowers are the joy of the whole wide
    earth,
Sweet nature's laughter and secret tears—
Whoso hearkens a bird in its spring-time
    mirth
The song of a flow'r-soul hears !

SONG OF THE CORNFIELDS

For miles along the sunlit lands
We sway in waves of gold,
A yellow sea that past the strands
Has inland rolled.

The sweet dews feed us thro' the night,
The soft winds blow around ;
The dayshine gladdens us with light
And stores the ground.

We feed a thousand happy birds,
The field-mice have their share—
Surely to these the reaping swords
Some grains can spare.

The deep joy of the joyous earth,
We feel it throb and thrill ;
The sweet return of natural mirth,
Spring's miracle.

All lands rejoice in us, we have
A glory such as kings
Might envy—but our gold we wave
For humbler things.

Song of the Cornfields

Our golden harvest is for those
Who strive and toil through life,
Who feel its agonies, its throes,
Its want, its strife.

O'er all the broad lands 'neath the sun,
We spring, we ripen, glow ;
The seasons change, the swift days run,—
Again we grow.

THE FIELD MOUSE

When the moon shines o'er the corn
And the beetle drones his horn,
And the flittermice swift fly,
And the nightjars swooping cry,
And the young hares run and leap,
We waken from our sleep.

And we climb with tiny feet
And we munch the green corn sweet
With startled eyes for fear
The white owl should fly near,
Or long slim weasel spring
Upon us where we swing.

We do no hurt at all :
Is there not room for all
Within the happy world ?
All day we lie close curled
In drowsy sleep, nor rise
Till through the dusky skies
The moon shines o'er the corn,
And the beetle drones his horn.

THE WEST WIND

I come from out the West,
And I breathe a breath of rest,
And the sweet birds greet me singing
From every tiny nest.

I am the wind of flow'rs—
I haunt the wild-wood bow'rs—
And when my song is ringing
Spring knows her sweetest hours.

But when the autumn days
Grow short, I rise and race
Thro' all the woodlands, flinging
Strewn leaves o'er every place.

When winter comes once more,
With deëp tumultuous roar
I sweep o'er ocean, bringing
Wild tempests to each shore.

HYMN OF THE FORESTS

We are the harps which the winds play,
A myriad tones in one vast sound
That the earth hearkens night and day—
A ceaseless music swaying round
The whole wide world, each voiceful tree
Echoing the wave-chants of the sea.

For even as inland waves that moan
But break not 'midst the unflowing green
Our trees are : and when tempests groan
And howl our frantic boughs between,
Our tumult is as when the deep
Struggles with winds that o'er it sweep.

'Neath bitter northern skies we stand,
Silent amidst the unmelting snows,
Gaunt warders of the desolate land :
Silent, save when the keen wind blows
The drifting wreaths about our feet,
Then moan we mournful music sweet.

Or in vast ancient woods of beech
Far south we make Spring's dearest home
The haunt of myriad songsters, each
A living flow'r made free to roam

Hymn of the Forests

From bough to bough, and thence we send
A forest-music without end.

'Neath tropic suns and ceaseless glow
With orient splendours we are filled :
'Midst Austral solitudes we grow,
Where seldom human voice has thrilled :
And ever and where'er we rise
We chant our ancient harmonies.

For aye the sea sings loud and long
In strange and solemn mystery
A wonderful transmitted song—
The echo of all history—
This song o'er all earth's lands we sing
While round the circling seasons swing.

SONG OF THE DESERTS

Wide, open, free, unbounded, vast,
We leagueless stretch the wide world o'er :
Above us sweeps the desert blast,
Or booms the lion's reverberate roar
Or the long howl of wolves that race
Like shadows o'er the moonlit space
In tireless, swift, relentless chase.

We are the haunt of all the winds,
O'er us as o'er the sea they sweep
In boundless freedom : each blast finds
A leagueless waste whereo'er to leap
And race unchecked,—and day and night
We hear the wild rush of their flight,
A desert-music infinite.

Ten thousand leagues of grassy plain
We stretch, or trackless wastes of sand :
O'er us no mortal king doth reign,
But Bedouin or savage band
And wild-eyed beasts of prey alone
Wander about our tameless zone ;
That bondage never yet hath known.

A RECORD

(*A Fragment*)

For, God wot, not the less a thing is true
Though every wight may not it chance to see.
CHAUCER.

I hear the dark tempestuous sea
Boom through the night monotonously,
The hoarse faint cry of breaking waves
Lashed by the wind that moans and raves
Upon the deep—I hear them fall
Against cliff-bases smooth and tall,
A music wild, funereal.

I seem to listen to a sound
That circles earth for ever round,
The dirge of an eternal song,
A dull deep music swept along
The listening coasts of many lands,
Sighed mournfully o'er level sands,
Or thunder'd amidst rocky strands.

I sit within my lonely room
Where the lamp's flame just breaks the
    gloom,

67

A Record

And thro' the darkness of the night
I see far down a starry light
Where nestled safely in the chine
The village street in one long line
Doth like a glittering serpent shine.

The keen wind blows through the dark
    skies,
The stars look down like countless eyes
That see and know, and therefore stare
Unmoved 'midst their serene high air :
And life seems but a dream, a shade
Which fleeting Time o'er space hath laid,
But which with Time shall one day fade.

Old memories are mine once more,
I see strange lives I lived of yore ;
With dimmed sight see I far-off things,
I feel the breath of bygone springs,
And ringing strangely in mine ears
I hear old laughter, alien tears
Slow falling, voices of past years.

Far back the soul can never see—
But dreams restore mysteriously
Dim visions of a possible past,
A time ere the last bond was cast
Aside that bound the struggling soul
Unto the brute, and first some goal
Loomed dimly over Life's vast shoal.

A Record

And dreaming so I live my dream :
I see a yellow turbid stream
Heavily flowing through clustered weeds
Of tropic growth, and 'midst the reeds
Of tall green rice upon its bank
A crouching tiger, long and lank,
With slow tail swaying from flank to flank.

Its eyes are yellow flames, and burn
Upon a man who dips an urn
Into the Ganges' sacred wave,
Unknowing he has reached his grave—
A short, hoarse roar, a scream, a blow !
And even as I shudder, lo,
My tiger-selt I seem to know.

And dreaming so I live my dream :
I see a sunrise glory gleam
Against vast mountain-heights, and there
Upon a peak precipitous, bare,
I see an eagle scan the plain
Immeasurable of his domain,
With fierce untamable disdain :

When first the stars wax pale his eyes
Front the wide east where day doth rise,
And with unflinching gaze look straight
Against the sun, then proud, elate,
On tireless wings he swoops on high

A Record

O'er countless leagues, and thro' the sky
Drifts like a dark cloud ominously :

Then as day dies and swift night springs,
I hear the sudden rush of wings
And see the eagle from the plain
Sweep to his eyrie once again
With fierce keen dauntless eyes aglow—
And even as I watch them, lo,
Mine eagle-self I seem to know.

And dreaming so I live my dream :
I hear a savage voice, a scream
Scarcely articulate, and far
I see a red light like a star
Flashed 'neath old trees, and the first fire
Made by the brutish tribe burn higher
Until unfed its flames expire :

I see the savage whose hand drew
The fire from wood, whose swift breath blew
The flame until it gained new strength,—
I see him stand supreme at length,
And pointing to the burning flame
Bend low his swart and trembling frame
And cry aloud a guttural name :

A god at last the tribe hath found,
A god at whose strange crackling sound

A Record

Each man must bend in dread until
This strange new god hath worked his will :
But lo, one day the fire spread fast,
And ere its fury is o'erpast
The tribe within its furnace-blast

Hath perish'd, save one man alone
Who far in sudden fear hath flown :
But with a gleam of new-born thought
A second flame he soon hath wrought
Only to tramp it down, aware
At last that no dead god lies there,
Or one for whom no man need care.

He looks around to see some god,
And far upon the fire-scorch'd sod
He sees his brown-burnt tribesmen lie,
And thinks their voices fill the sky,
And dreads some unseen sudden blow—
And even as I watch him, lo,
My savage-self I seem to know.

And dreaming so I live my dream :
I see a flood of moonlight gleam
Between vast ancient oaks, and round
A rough-hewn altar on the ground
Weird Druid priests are gatherèd
While through their midst a man is led
With face that is already dead :

A Record

A low chant swells throughout the wood,
Then comes a solemn interlude
Ere loudlier rings dim aisles along
Some ancient sacrificial song ;
Before the fane the victim kneels
And without sound he forward reels
When the priest's knife the death-blow deals:

The moonlight falls upon his face,
His blood is spatter'd o'er the place,
But now he is ev'n as a flow'r
Uprooted in some tempest hour,
Dead, but whose seed shall elsewhere grow :
And as I look upon him, lo,
Some old ancestral-self I know.

Thus far dreams bring mysteriously
Visions of past lives back to me ;
Visions alone perhaps they are,
Each one a wandering futile star
Flash'd o'er the mental firmament,—
Yet may be thus in past times went
My soul in gradual ascent.

None sees the slow sure upward sweep
By which the soul from life-depths deep
Ascends—unless, mayhap, when free
With each new death we backward see

A Record

The long perspective of our race,
Our multitudinous past lives trace
Since first as breath of God through space

Each came, and filled the lowest thing
With life's faint pulse scarce quivering ;
So ever onward upward grew,
And ever with each death-birth knew
An old sphere left, a mystic change—
A sense of exaltation strange
Thus through a myriad lives to range.

But even in our mortal lives
At times the eager spirit strives
To gain through subtle memories
Some hint of life's past mysteries—
Brief moments they, that flash before
Bewilder'd eyes some scene of yore,
Some vivid hour returned once more.

Swift through the darken'd clouds of
 sense
A sudden lightning-gleam intense
Reveals some glimpse of the long past,
Some memory comes back at last—
And yet 'twas but a sudden strain
Of song—a scent—a sound of rain—
Some trifle—made all clear again.

73

A Record

With a swift glance such glimpses come
And go—but there are times for some
When keen the vision is, so keen
That thenceforth the indelible scene
Remains within the mind for aye,
Some reminiscence sad or gay,
Some action of a bygone day.

Thus came to me memorious gleams
From the closed past, no sleep-brought
    dreams
But revelations flashed out swift
Upon the mind : a sudden lift
Of the dense cloud of all past years,—
A moment when the thrilling ears
Heard, or the eyes slow filled with tears.

Thus has there flashed across my sight
A desert in a blinding light
Of scorching sun, a dreary waste
Of burning sand where seldom paced
The swift, gaunt camels with their freight
Of merchandise, but where the weight
Of silence lay inviolate.

There a few sterile rocks lay white
In the sun's glare, a band by might
Of old convulsions thither hurl'd
In the far days of the young world :

74

A Record

And in their midst a hollow cave
Was cleft, where dwelt, as in a grave,
One who came thence his soul to save.

Young, and from out the joyous strife
Of men he came to this drear life :
No more for him the wine's swift spell,
No more for him love's miracle—
But bitter as the dead sea's dust
Seem'd all past joys—dread things to thrust
Aside, all equally accursed.

In fervid prayer all day he sought
God's grace : in dreams at night he fought
The fierce temptations born of youth.
Awake, he strove to reach God's truth—
Asleep, he felt his passions rise
And darken all the heav'nly skies
With dread deceitful lovely lies.

Thus year by year he fell and rose
In endless conflict, till his woes
Fill'd all his days with burning tears
And dreadful never-ending fears :
Haggard he grew from scanty food,
With sun and blast and shelter rude
And terrors of his lonelihood.

With long hair streaming out behind
He raced before the burning wind,
With wild insane strained eyes alert

75

A Record

For demons lurking to his hurt—
And though the sun beat fiercely hot
Upon the sands, he heeded not
But like a wand'ring shadow shot

Across the burning level waste,
Oft shouting as he wildly raced
" My body is in hell, but I,
Its soul, thus hither speed and cry
To God to blow me as a leaf
From out this agony of grief,
To slay, and give me death's relief ! "

Oft as he fled, with from his mouth
The white froth blown- thro' maddening
        drought,
He pass'd the crouching lion's lair—
But when his shrill laugh fill'd the air
The desert monarch shrank, as though
He feared this raving shadow's woe,
This haggard wretch with eyes aglow.

But when the sun sank past the west
The hermit fled the desert, lest
God's eyes should lose him in the night,
And foes Satanic guide his flight
Till soul and body once again
Made one should with the pangs of twain,
In hell for ever writhe in pain.

A Record

But when sleep came to him he lay
In peace, and oft a smile would play
Upon his face as though once more
In dreams he lived his life of yore,—
The life he did himself dismiss,
The old sweet time of joy and bliss,—
Heard laughter, or felt some loved kiss.

Thus have I seen, and seeing known
That he who lived afar alone,
A hermit on a dreary waste,
Was even that soul mine eyes have traced
Through brute and savage steadily,
That he even now is part of me
Just as a wave is of the sea.

*   *   *   *

Far out across the deep doth swell
The hoarse boom of the Black-Rock bell,
A heavy moan monotonous,
An inner sea-sound ominous,
As though throughout the ocean there
Relentless Conscience aye did bear
A bitter message of despair.

Still sweeps the old impetuous sea
Around the green earth ceaselessly—
Changeless, yet full of change, it seems
The very mirror of those dreams

A Record

We call men's lives—for are not they
Like life-sea waves Fate's winds doth sway
And break, yet which pass not away

Through depth of silent air, but blend
Once more with the deep and lend
Their never dying music sweet
To the great choral song complete ;
Each death is but a birth, a change—
Each soul through myriad by-ways strange,
Through birth and death, doth upward
  range.

MOONRISE FROM IONA

Here, where in dim forgotten days
A savage people chanted lays
To long since perished gods, I stand :
The sea breaks in, runs up the sand,
Retreats as with a long-drawn sigh,
Sweeps in again ; again leaves dry
The ancient beach, so old and yet
So new that as the strong tides fret
The island barriers in their flow
The ebb-hours of each day can know
A surface change. The day is dead,
The sun is set, and overhead
The white north stars shine keen and bright ;
The wind upon the sea is light
And just enough to stir the deep
With phosphorescent gleams and sweep
The spray from salt waves as they rise :
And yonder light—is't from the skies
Some meteor strange, a burning star—
Or a lamp hung upon a spar
Of vessel undescribed ?   It gleams
And rises slowly, till it seems

79

Moonrise from Iona

A burning isle, an angel-throne
Reset on earth, a mountain-cone
Of gold new-risen from sea-caves—
Until at last above the waves,
Salt with Atlantic brine, it swims
A silver crescent.   Now no hymns
In the wild Runic speech are heard,
No chant, no sacrificial word :
But only moans the weary sea,
And only the cold wind sings free,
And where the Runic temples stood
The bat flies and the owl doth brood.

MOONRISE ON THE VENETIAN LAGOONS

A more than twilight darkness dwells
Upon the long lagoons : the bells
Of distant Venice come and go
Like sounds in dreams ; the tide's soft flow
Sweeps onward, and a wandering gull
Flits o'er the track of yon black hull
Just fading in the gloom—no more
I see or hear 'tween shore and shore :
But as I lie and dreamily
Watch the dark water from the sea
Slip past the boat, in its blurred sky
I see the crescent moon on high
Casting curv'd golden flakes far down
Amidst the calm lagoon—a crown
Broken innumerably up,
The gold bands of a broken cup.
I take an oar and make a rift
In the soft tide of the lagoons,—
And lo, the blade itself doth lift
A score of quivering crescent moons,
And as they flash I seem to see
Each droplet with a small moon flee.

MOONRISE ON THE ANTARCTIC

The huge white icebergs silently
Voyage with us through this lonely sea,
Noiseless and lifeless, yet they seem
Like haunted islands in a dream
Holding strange secrets that no one
May know and live.   In the bright sun
They shine immeasurably fair,
Bluer than bluest summer air,
Or clear to the very heart with green
Pure light, or amethyst as seen
'Mid sunset-clouds—but now they shine
With a cold gleam and have no sign
Of loveliness.   The ship swings on,
Plunging 'mid surging seas whereon
Few vessels ever sail, and as
Slowly the long hours come and pass
The late moon rises cold and white,
And sends a flood of wintry light
Along the sweeping waves and round
Our black and sea-worn hull.   A sound
Far off dies while it grows—some seal
Long-drifted, frozen, waking but to feel
Death's grip.   And now the spectral isles

Moonrise on the Antarctic

Grow whiter, icier still, and seem
More hollow, with a strange weird gleam
As though some pale unreal fires
Consumed them to their utmost spires
Yet without flame or heat. And still
The moon doth rise, and seems to fill
Each berg anew with life : we sail
Upon a strange sad sea, where pale
And moonshine isles float all around,
Voyaging onward without sound.

TRANSCRIPTS
FROM NATURE

(FROM "THE HUMAN INHERITANCE"
AND "EARTH'S VOICES")

1882–1886

WILD ROSES

Against the dim hot summer blue
  Yon wave of white wild-roses lies,
  Watching with listless golden eyes
The green leaves shutting out their view,
  The tiny leaves whose motions bright
  Are like small wings of emerald light :

White butterflies like snow-flakes fall
And brown bees drone their honey-call.

THE EBBING TIDE

A long low gurgle down the strand,
  The sputtering of the drying wrack !
  The tide is slowly ebbing back
With listless murmuring from the land,
  And the small waves reluctant flow
  Where the broad-bosomed currents go.

The sea has fall'n asleep, and lies
Dense blue beneath the dense blue skies.

DAWN AMID SCOTCH FIRS

The furtive lights that herald dawn
   Are shimmering 'mid the steel-blue firs ;
   A slow awakening wind half stirs
And the long branches breathe upon ;
   The east grows clearer—clearer—lo,
   The day is born ! A refluent flow

Of silver waves along each tree
For one brief moment dazzlingly.

A DEAD CALM AND MIST

(Towards evening)

The slow heave of the sleeping sea
   With pulse-like motion swells and falls,
   And drowsily a stray gull calls
The very wail of melancholy ;
   All day the moveless mist has slept
   On the same bosom east winds swept :

No breath of change in the grey mist,
Save just a dream of amethyst.

TANGLED SUNRAYS

Aslant from yonder sunlit hill
  The lance-like sunrays stream across
  The meadows where the king-cups toss
I' the wind, and where the beech-leaves thrill
  With flooding light they twist and turn
  And seem to interlace and burn,

Until at last in tangle spun
'Mid the damp grass their race is run.

LOCH CORUISK (SKYE)

The bleak and barren mountains keep
  A never-ending gloom around
  The lonely loch ; the winds resound,
The rains beat down, the tempests sweep,
  The days are calm and dark and still,—
  No other changes Coruisk fill.

Scarce living sound is heard, save high
The eagle's scream or wild swan's cry.

SUNRISE ABOVE BROAD WHEAT-FIELDS

The pale tints of the twilight fields
  Have turnèd into burnished gold,
  For waves of yellow light have rolled
From the open'd east across the wealds ;
  While 'mid the wheat spires far behind
  Stirs lazily the awaken'd wind.

A skylark high (a song-made bird)
Sings as though God his singing heard.

PHOSPHORESCENT SEA

The sea scarce heaves in its calm sleep,
  The wind has not awakened yet
  Tho' in its dreams it seems to fret ;
For, ever and again, the deep
  Hearkens a sigh that steals along
  As might some echo of sad song :

Ah, there the wind stirs ! Lo, the dark
Dim sea's on fire around our barque.

90

A GREEN WAVE

Between the salt sea-send before
And all the flowing gulfs behind,
  Half lifted by the rising wind,
Half eager for the ungain'd shore,
  A great green wave of shining light
  Sweeps onward crowned with dazzling
    white :

Above, the east wind shreds the sky
With plumes from the grey clouds that fly.

A CRYSTAL FOREST

The air is blue and keen and cold,
  With snow the roads and fields are white ;
  But here the forest's clothed with light
And in a shining sheath enrolled.
  Each branch, each twig, each blade of
    grass,
  Seems clad miraculously with glass :

Above the ice-bound streamlet bends
Each frozen fern with crystal ends.

91

THE WASP

Where the ripe pears droop heavily
  The yellow wasp hums loud and long
  His hot and drowsy autumn song :
A yellow flame he seems to be,
  When darting suddenly from high
  He lights where fallen peaches lie :

Yellow and black, this tiny thing's
A tiger-soul on elfin wings.

AN AUTUMNAL EVENING

Deep black against the dying glow
  The tall elms stand ; the rooks are still ;
  No windbreath makes the faintest thrill
Amongst the leaves ; the fields below
  Are vague and dim in twilight shades—
  Only the bats wheel in their raids

On the grey flies, and silently
Great dusky moths go flitting by.

A WINTER HEDGEROW

The wintry wolds are white ; the wind
  Seems frozen ; in the shelter'd nooks
  The sparrows shiver ; the black rooks
Wheel homeward where the elms behind
  The manor stand ; at the field's edge
  The redbreasts in the blackthorn hedge

Sit close and under snowy eaves
The shrewmice sleep 'mid nested leaves.

THE ROOKERY AT SUNRISE

The lofty elm-trees darkly dream
  Against the steel-blue sky ; till far
  I' the twilit east a golden star
O'erbrims the dusk in one vast stream
  Of yellow light, and lo ! a cry
  Breaks from the windy nest—the sky

Is filled with wheeling rooks—they sway
In one black phalanx towards the day.

93

MOONRISE

The first snows of the year lie white
　Upon the branches bending low ;
　A surging wind the flakes doth blow
Before the coming feet of Night—
　Half dusk, half day, betwixt the pines
　Green-yellow the full moon reclines :

Green-yellow, and now wholly green,
While faint the windy stars are seen.

FIREFLIES

Softly sailing emerald lights
　Above the cornfields come and go,
　Listlessly wandering to and fro :
The magic of these July nights
　Has surely even pierced down deep
　Where the earth's jewels unharmed sleep,

And filled with fire the emeralds there
And raised them thus to the outer air.

94

THE CRESCENT MOON

As though the Power that made the nautilus
 A living glory o'er seas perilous
 Scathless to roam, had from the utmost
  deep
Called a vast flawless pearl from out its sleep
 And carv'd it crescent-wise, exceeding
  fair,—
 So seems the crescent moon that thro' the
  air

With motionless motion glides from out the
 west,
And sailing onward ever seems at rest.

THE EAGLE

Between two mighty hills a sheer
 Abyss—far down in the ravine
 A thread-like torrent and a screen
Of oaks like shrubs—and one doth rear
 A dry scarp'd peak above all sound
 Save windy voices wailing round :

At sunrise here, in proud disdain
The eagle scans his vast domain.

A VENETIAN SUNSET : BEFORE A CHANGE

(Returning from Torcello)

In violet hues each dome and spire
　Stands outlined against flawless rose ;
　O'er this a carmine ocean flows
Streak'd with pure gold and amber fire,
　And through the sea of sundown mist
　Float isles of melted amethyst :

Storm-portents, saffron streamers rise,
Fan-like, from Venice to the skies,

EMPIRE (PERSEPOLIS)

The yellow waste of yellow sands,
　The bronze haze of a scorching sky !
　Lo, what are these that broken lie ;
Were these once temples made with hands ?
　Once towers and palaces that knew
　No hint of that which one day threw

Their greatness to the winds—made this
The memory of Persepolis ?

AUSTRALIAN SKETCHES

THE LAST ABORIGINAL

I see him sit, wild-eyed, alone,
Amidst gaunt, spectral, moonlit gums—
He waits for death : not once a moan
From out his rigid fixt lips comes ;
His lank hair falls adown a face
Haggard as any wave-worn stone,
And in his eyes I dimly trace
The memory of a vanished race.

The lofty ancient gum-trees stand,
Each grey and ghostly in the moon,
The giants of an old strange land
That was exultant in its noon
When all our Europe was o'erturned
With deluge and with shifting sand,
With earthquakes that the hills inurned
And central fires that fused and burned.

The moon moves slowly through the vast
And solemn skies ; the night is still,
Save when a warrigal springs past
With dismal howl, or when the shrill

The last Aboriginal

Scream of a parrot rings which feels
A twining serpent's fangs fixt fast,
Or when a grey opossum squeals,
Or long iguana, as it steals

From bole to bole disturbs the leaves :
But hush'd and still he sits—who knows
That all is o'er for him who weaves
With inner speech, malign, morose,
A curse upon the whites who came
And gather'd up his race like sheaves
Of thin wheat, fit but for the flame—
Who shot or spurned them without shame.

He knows he shall not see again
The creeks whereby the lyre-birds sing—
He shall no more upon the plain,
Sun scorch'd, and void of water-spring,
Watch the dark cassowaries sweep
In startled flight, or, with spear lain
In ready poise, glide, twist, and creep
Where the brown kangaroo doth leap.

No more in silent dawns he'll wait
By still lagoons, and mark the flight
Of black swans near : no more elate
Whirl high the boomerang aright
Upon some foe : he knows that now
He too must share his race's night—
He scarce can know the white man's plough
Will one day pass above his brow.

The last Aboriginal

Last remnant of the Austral race
He sits and stares, with failing breath :
The shadow deepens on his face,
For 'midst the spectral gums waits death.
A dingo's sudden howl swells near—
He stares once with a startled gaze,
As half in wonder, half in fear,
Then sinks back on his unknown bier.

THE COROBBOREE

(*Midnight*)

Deep in the forest-depths the tribe
A mighty blazing fire have made :
Round this they spring with frantic yells
In hideous pigments all arrayed—

One barred with yellow ochre, one
A skeleton in startling white,
There one who dances furiously
Blood-red against the great fire's light,—

With death's insignia on his breast,
In rude design, the swart chief springs ;
And loud and long each echoes back
The savage war-cry that he sings.

Within the forest dark and dim
The startled cockatoos like ghosts
Flit to and fro, the mopokes scream,
And parrots rise in chattering hosts ;

The Corobboree

The gins and lubras crouch and watch
With eager shining brute-like eyes,
And ever and again shrill back
Wild echoes of the frantic cries :—

Like some infernal scene it is—
The forest dark, the blazing fire,
The ghostly birds, the dancing fiends,
Whose savage chant swells ever higher.

Afar away gaunt wild-dogs howl,
And strange cries vaguely call : but white
The placid moon sails on, and flame
The silent stars above the night.

JUSTICE

(Uncivilised and Civilised)

Ling-Tso Ah Sin, on Murderer's Flat
One morning caught an old grey rat :
" Ah, white man, I have got you now !
But no—dust be upon my brow
If needless blood I cause to fall—
So go, there's world-room for us all ! "

That night Ah Sin was somehow shot—
By *accident !* For he had got
From earth a little gold—black sin
For *thee*, though not for us, Ah Sin !

MURDERER'S FLAT, *February* 1878.

NOON-SILENCE

(Australian Forest)

A lyre-bird sings a low melodious song—
Then all is still : a soft wind breathes along
The lofty gums and faintly dies away :
And Silence wakes and knows her dream is
    day.

AUSTRALIAN
TRANSCRIPTS

I. AN ORANGE GROVE

(Victoria)

The short sweet purple twilight dreams
Of vanish'd day, of coming night ;
And like gold moons in the soft light
Each scented drooping orange gleams
From out the glossy leaves black-green
That make through noon a cool dark screen.
   The dusk is silence, save the thrill
   That stirs it from cicalas shrill.

II. BLACK SWANS ON THE
MURRAY LAGOONS

The long lagoons lie white and still
Beneath the great round Austral moon :
The sudden dawn will waken soon
With many a delicious thrill :
Between this death and life the cries
Of black swans ring through silent skies—
   And the long wash of the slow stream
   Moves as in sleep some bodeful dream.

III. BREAKING BILLOWS AT SORRENTO

(Victoria)

A sky of whirling flakes of foam,
A rushing world of dazzling blue:
One moment, the sky looms in view—
The next, a crash in its curved dome,
A tumult indescribable,
And eyes dazed with the miracle.
  Here breaks by circling day and night
  In thunder the sea's boundless might.

IV. SHEA-OAK TREES ON A STORMY DAY

(S.E. Victoria)

O'er sandy tracts the shea-oak trees
Droop their long wavy grey-green trails :
And inland wandering moans and wails
The long blast of the ocean-breeze :
Like loose strings of a viol or harp
These answering sound—now low, now sharp
  And keen, a melancholy strain :
  A death song o'er the mournful plain.

V. MID-NOON IN JANUARY

Upon a fibry fern-tree bough
A huge iguana lies alow,
Bright yellow in the noonday glow
With bars of black,—it watcheth now
A gorgeous insect hover high
Till suddenly its lance doth fly
    And catch the prey—but still no sound
    Breathes 'mid the green fern-spaces round.

VI. IN THE FERN

(Gippsland)

The feathery fern-trees make a screen
Where through the sunglare cannot pass—
Fern, gum, and lofty sassafras :
The fronds sweep over, palely green,
And underneath are orchids curl'd
Adream through this cool shadow-world ;
    A fragrant greenness—like the noon
    Of lime-tree in an English June.

VII. SUNSET AMID THE BUFFALO MOUNTAINS

(N.E. Victoria)

Across the boulder'd majesty
Of the great hills the passing day
Drifts like a wind-borne cloud away
Far off beyond the western sky :
And while a purple glory spreads,
With straits of gold and brilliant reds,
  An azure veil, translucent, strange,
  Dreamlike steals over each dim range.

VIII. THE FLYING MOUSE

(New South Wales—Moonlight)

The eucalyptus-blooms are sweet
With honey, and the birds all day
Sip the clear juices forth : brown-grey,
A bird-like thing with tiny feet
Cleaves to the boughs, or with small wings
Amidst the leafy spaces springs,
  And in the moonshine with shrill cries
  Flits batlike where the white gums rise.

IX. THE BELL-BIRD

The stillness of the Austral noon
Is broken by no single sound—
No lizards even on the ground
Rustle amongst dry leaves—no tune
The lyre-bird sings—yet hush ! I hear
A soft bell tolling, silvery clear !
  Low soft aerial chimes, unknown
  Save 'mid these silences alone.

X. THE WOOD-SWALLOWS *

(Sunrise)

The lightning-stricken giant gum
Stands leafless, dead—a giant still
But heedless of this sunrise-thrill :
What stir is this where all was dumb ?—
What seem like old dead leaves break swift,
And lo, a hundred wings uplift
  A cloud of birds that to and fro
  Dart joyous midst the sunrise-glow.

* The wood-swallows of Australia have the singular
habit of clustering like bees or bats on the boughs of
a dead tree.

XI. THE ROCK-LILY

(New South Wales)

The amber-tinted level sands
Unbroken stretch for leagues away
Beyond these granite slabs, dull grey
And lifeless, herbless—save where stands
The mighty rock-flow'r towering high,
With carmine blooms crowned gloriously :
  A giant amongst flowers it reigns,
  The glory of these Austral plains.

XII. THE FLAME-TREE

(New South Wales)

For miles the Illawarra range
Runs level with Pacific seas :
What glory when the morning breeze
Upon its slopes doth shift and change
Deep pink and crimson hues, till all
The leagues-long distance seems a wall
  Of swift uncurling flames of fire
  That wander not nor reach up higher.

FROM

ROMANTIC BALLADS

1888

THE WEIRD OF MICHAEL SCOTT

The wild wind moaned : fast waned the
    light :
Dense cloud-wrack gloomed the front of
    night :
The moorland cries were cries of pain :
Green, red, or broad and glaring white
    The lightnings flashed athwart the main.

The sound and fury of the waves,
Upon the rocks, among the caves,
    Boomed inland from the thunderous
    strand :
Mayhap the dead heard in their graves
    The tumult fill the hollow land.

With savage pebbly rush and roar
The billows swept the echoing shore
    In clouds of spume and swirling spray :
The wild wings of the tempest bore
    The salt rheum to the Haunted Brae.

The Weird of Michael Scott

Upon the Haunted Brae (where none
Would linger in the noontide sun)
   Michael the Wizard rode apace :
Wildly he rode where all men shun,
   With madness gleaming on his face.

Loud, loud he laugh'd whene'er he saw
The lightnings split on Lammer-Law,
   " Blood, bride, and bier the auld rune saith
Hell's wind tae me ae nicht sall blaw,
   The nicht I ride unto my death ! "

Across the Haunted Brae he fled,
And mock'd and jeer'd the shuddering pead ;
   Wan white the horse that he bestrode,
The fire-flaughts stricken as it sped
   Flashed thro' the black mirk of the road.

And even as his race he ran,
A shade pursued the fleeing man,
   A white and ghastly shade it was ;
" Like saut sea-spray across wet san'
   Or wind abune the moonlit grass !—

" Like saut sea-spray it follows me,
Or wind o'er grass—so fast's I flee :
   In vain I shout, and laugh, and call—
The thing betwixt me and the sea
   God kens it is my ain lost saul ! "

The Weird of Michael Scott

Down, down the Haunted Brae, and past
The verge of precipices vast
  And eyries where the eagles screech ;
By great pines swaying in the blast,
    Through woods of moaning larch and
      beech ;

On, on by moorland glen and stream,
Past lonely lochs where ospreys scream,
  Past marsh-lands where no sound is
    heard,
The rider and his white horse gleam,
  And, aye behind, that dreadful third.

Wild and more wild the wild wind blew,
But Michael Scott the rein ne'er drew :
  Loud and more loud his laughter shrill,
His wild and mocking laughter, grew,
  In dreadful cries 'twixt hill and hill.

At last the great high road he gained,
And now with whip and voice he strained
  To swifter flight the gleaming mare ;
Afar ahead the fierce sleet rained
  Upon the ruin'd House of Stair.

Then Michael Scott laughed long and loud :
" Whan shone the mune ahint yon cloud
  I kent the Towers that saw my birth—
Lang, lang, sall wait my cauld grey shroud,
  Lang cauld and weet my bed o' earth ! "

The Weird of Michael Scott

But as by Stair he rode full speed
His horse began to pant and bleed :
    " Win hame, win hame, my bonnie mare,
Win hame if thou would'st rest and feed,
    Win hame, we're nigh the House of Stair ! "

But with a shrill heart-bursten yell
The white horse stumbled, plunged, and fell,
    And loud a summoning voice arose,
" Is't White-Horse Death that rides frae
      Hell,
    Or Michael Scott that hereby goes ? "

" Ah, Lord of Stair, I ken ye weel !
Avaunt, or I your saul sall steal,
    An' send ye howling through the wood
A wild man-wolf—aye, ye maun reel
    An' cry upon your Holy Rood ! "

Swift swept the sword within the shade,
Swift was the flash the blue steel made,
    Swift was the downward stroke and rash—
But, as though leven-struck, the blade
    Fell splintered earthward with a crash.

With frantic eyes Lord Stair out-peered
When Michael Scott laughed loud and
      jeered :—
    " Forth fare ye now, ye've gat lang room !

The Weird of Michael Scott

Ah, by my saul thou'lt dree thy weird !
  Begone, were-wolf, till the day o' doom ! "

A shrill scream pierced the lonely place ;
A dreadful change came o'er the face ;
  The head, with bristled hair, swung low ;
Michael the Wizard turned and fled
  And laughed a mocking laugh of woe.

And through the wood there stole and crept,
And through the wood there raced and leapt,
  A thing in semblance of a man ;
An awful look its wild eyes kept
  As howling through the night it ran.

PART II

Athwart the wan bleak moonlit waste,
With staring eyes, in frantic haste,
With thin locks back-blown by the wind,
A grey gaunt haggard figure raced
And moaned the thing that sped behind.

It followed him, afar or near :
In wrath he curs'd ; he shrieked in fear ;
But ever more it followed him :
Eftsoons he'd stop, and turn, and peer
To front the following phantom grim.

The Weird of Michael Scott

Naught would he see ; in vain would list
For wing-like sound or feet that hissed
Like wind-blown snow upon the ice ;
The grey thing vanished like a mist,
Or like the smoke of sacrifice :

" Come forth frae out the mirk," his cry,
" For I maun live or I maun die,
But na, nae mair I'll suffer baith ! "
Then, with a shriek, would onward fly
And, swift behind, his following wraith.

Michael the Wizard sped across
The peat and bracken o' the moss :
He heard the muir-wind rise and fall,
And laughed to see the birk-boughs toss
An' the stealthy shadows leap or crawl.

When white St. Monan's Water streamed
For leagues athwart the muir, and gleamed
With phosphorescent marish-fires,
With wild and sudden joy he screamed,
For scarce a mile was Kevan-Byres—

Sweet Kevan-Byres, dear Kevan-Byres,
That oft of old was thronged with squires
And joyous damsels blithe and gay :
Alas, alas for Kevan-Byres
That now is cold and grey.

The Weird of Michael Scott

There in bed on linen sheet
With white soft limbs and love-dreams sweet
Fair Margaret o' the Byres would be :
(Ah, when he'd lain and kissed her feet
Had she not laughed in mockery !)

Aye she had laughed, for what reck'd she
O' a' the powers of Wizardie !
" Win up, win up, guid Michael Scott,
For ye sall ne'er win boon o' me,
By plea, or sword, or spell, God wot ! "

Aye, these the words that she had said :
These were the words that as he fled
Michael the Wizard muttered o'er—
" My Margaret, bow your bonnie head,
For ye sall never flout me more ! "

Swiftly he raced, with gleaming eyes,
And wild, strange, sobbing, panting cries,
Dire, dire, and fell his frantic mood ;
Until he gained St. Monan's Rise
Whereon the House of Kevan stood.

There looked he long and fixed his gaze
Upon a room where in past days
His very soul had pled love's boon :
Lit was it now with the wan rays
Flick-flickering from the cloud-girt moon.

The Weird of Michael Scott

"Come forth, May Margaret, come, my
        heart !
For thou and I nae mair sall part—
Come forth, I bid, though Christ himsel'
My bitter love should strive to thwart,
For I have a' the powers o' hell ! "

What was the white wan thing that came
And lean'd from out the window-frame,
And waved wild arms against the sky ?
What was the hollow echoing name,
What was the thin despairing cry ?

Adown the long and dusky stair,
And through the courtyard bleak and bare,
And past the gate, and out upon
The whistling, moaning, midnight air—
What is't that Michael Scott has won !

Across the moat it seems to flee,
It speeds across the windy lea,
And through the ruin'd abbey-arch ;
Now like a mist all waveringly
It stands beneath a lonely larch.

"Come Margaret, my Margaret,
Thou see'st my vows I ne'er forget :
Come win wi' me across the waste—
Lang lang I've wandered cauld and wet,
An' now thy sweet warm lips would taste ! "

The Weird of Michael Scott

But as a whirling drift of snow,
Or flying foam the sea-winds blow,
Or smoke swept thin before a gale
It flew across the waste—and oh
'Twas Margaret's voice in that long wail !

Swift as the hound upon the deer,
Swift as the stag when nigh the mere,
Michael the Wizard followed fast—
What though May Margaret fled in fear,
She should be his, be his, at last !—

O'er broom and whin and bracken high,
Where the peat bog lay gloomily,
Where sullenly the bittern boomed
And startled curlews swept the sky,
Until St. Monan's Water loomed !

" The cauld wet water sall na be
The bride-bed for my love and me—
For now upon St. Monan's shore
May Margaret her love sall gie
To him she mocked and jeered of yore ! "

Was that a heron in its flight ?
Was that a mere-mist wan and white ?
What thing from lonely kirkyard grave ?
Forlorn it trails athwart the night
With arms that writhe and wring and wave !

The Weird of Michael Scott

Deep down within the mere it sank,
Among the slimy reeds and rank,
And all the leagues-long loch was bare—
One vast, grey, moonlit, lifeless blank
Beneath a silent waste of air.

" O God, O God ! her soul it is !
Christ's saved her frae my blasting kiss !
Her soul frae out her body drawn,
The body I maun have for bliss !
O body dead and spirit gaun ! "

Hours long o'er Monan's wave he stared ;
The fire-flaughts flashed and gleamed and
    glared,
The death-lights o' the lonely place :
And aye, dead still, he watch'd, till flared
The sunrise on his haggard face.

Full well he knew that with its fires
Loud was the tumult 'mong the squires,
And fierce the bitter pain of all
Where stark and stiff in Kevan-Byres
May Margaret lay beneath her pall.

Then once he laughed, and twice, and thrice,
Though deep within his hollow eyes
Dull-gleamed a light of fell despair.
Around, Earth grew a Paradise
In the sweet golden morning air.

The Weird of Michael Scott

Slowly he rose at last, and swift
One gaunt and frantic arm did lift
And curs'd God in his heav'n o'erhead :
Then, like a lonely cloud adrift,
Far from St. Monan's wave he fled.

PART III

All day the curlew wailed and screamed,
All day the cushat crooned and dreamed,
All day the sweet muir-wind blew free :
Beyond the grassy knowes far gleamed
The splendour of the singing sea.

Above the myriad gorse and broom
And miles of golden kingcup-bloom
The larks and yellowhammers sang :
Where the scaur cast an hour-long
    gloom
The lintie's liquid notes out-rang.

Oft as he wandered to and fro—
As idly as the foam-bells flow
Hither and thither on the deep—
Michael the Wizard's face would grow
From death to life, and he would
    weep—

The Weird of Michael Scott

Weep, weep wild tears of bitter pain
For what might never be again :
Yet even as he wept his face
Would gleam with mockery insane
And with fierce laughter on he'd race.

At times he watched the white clouds sail
Across the wastes of azure pale ;
Or oft would haunt some moorland pool
Fringed round with thyme and fragrant gale
And canna-tufts of snow-white wool.

Long in its depths would Michael stare,
As though some secret thing lay there :
Mayhap the moving water made
A gloom where crouched a Kelpie fair
With death-eyes gleaming through the shade.

Then on with weary listless feet
He fared afar, until the sweet
Cool sound of mountain brooks drew nigh,
And loud he heard the strayed lambs bleat
And the white ewes responsive cry.

High up among the hills full clear
He heard the belling of the deer
Amid the corries where they browsed,
And, where the peaks rose gaunt and sheer,
Fierce swirling echoes eagle-roused.

The Weird of Michael Scott

He watched the kestrel wheel and sweep,
He watched the dun fox glide and creep,
He heard the whaup's long-echoing call,
Watched in the stream the brown trout leap
And the grilse spring the waterfall.

Along the slopes the grouse-cock whirred ;
The grey-blue heron scarcely stirred
Amid the mossed grey tarn-side stones :
The burns gurg-gurgled through the yird
Their sweet clear bubbling undertones.

Above the tarn the dragon-fly
Shot like a flashing arrow by ;
And in a moving shifting haze
The gnat-clouds sank or soared on high
And danced their wild aërial maze.

As the day waned he heard afar
The hawking fern-owl's dissonant jar
Disturb the silence of the hill :
The gloaming came : star after star
He watched the skiey spaces fill.

But as the darkness grew and made
Forest and mountain one vast shade,
Michael the Wizard moaned in dread—
A long white moonbeam like a blade
Swept after him where'er he fled.

The Weird of Michael Scott

Swiftly he leapt o'er rock and root,
Swift o'er the fern his flying foot,
But swifter still the white moonbeam :
Wild was the grey-owl's dismal hoot,
But wilder still his maniac scream.

Once in his flight he paused to hear
A hollow shriek that echoed near :—
The louder were his dreadful cries,
The louder rang adown the sheer
Gaunt cliffs the echoing replies.

As though a hunted wolf, he raced
To the lone woods across the waste
Steep granite slopes of Crammond-Low—
The haunted forest where none faced
The terror that no man might know.

Betwixt the mountains and the sea
Dark leagues of pine stood solemnly,
Voiceful with grim and hollow song,
Save when each tempest-stricken tree
A savage tumult would prolong.

Beneath the dark funereal plumes,
Slow waving to and fro—death-blooms
Within the void dim wood of death—
Oft shuddering at the fearful glooms
Sped Michael Scott with failing breath.

The Weird of Michael Scott

Once, as he passed a dreary place,
Between two trees he saw a face—
A white face staring at his own :
A weird strange cry he gave for grace,
And heard an echoing moan.

" Whate'er ye be, O thing that bides
Among the trees—O thing that hides
In yonder moving mass o' shade
Come forth tae me ! "—wan Michael glides
Swift, as he speaks, athrough the glade :

" Whate'er ye be, I fear ye nought !
Michael the Wizard has na fought
Wi' men and demons year by year
To shirk ae thing he has na sought
Or blanch wi' any mortal fear ! "

But not a sound thrilled thro' the air—
Not even a she-fox in her lair
Or brooding bird made any stir—
All was as still and blank and bare
As is a vaulted sepulchre.

Then awe, and fear, and wild dismay
O'ercame mad Michael, ashy grey,
With eyes as of one newly dead :
" If wi' my sword I canna slay,
Ye'll dree my weird when it is said ! "

The Weird of Michael Scott

" Whate'er ye be, man, beast, or sprite,
I wind ye round wi' a sheet o' light—
Aye, round and round your burning frame
I cast by spell o' wizard might
A fierce undying sheet of flame ! "

Swift as he spoke a thing sprang out,
A man-like thing, all hemmed about
With blazing blasting burning fire !
The wind swoop'd wi' a demon-shout
And whirled the red flame higher and higher !

And as, appalled, wan Michael stood
The flying flaughts swift fired the wood ;
And even as he shook and stared
The gaunt pines turned the hue of blood
And all the waving branches flared.

Then with wild leaps the accursèd thing
Drew nigh and nigher : with a spring
Michael escaped its fiery clasp,
Although he felt the fierce flame sting
And all the horror of its grasp.

Swift as an arrow far he fled,
But swifter still the flames o'erhead
Rushed o'er the waving sea of pines,
And hollow noises crashed and sped
Like splitting blasts in ruin'd mines.

The Weird of Michael Scott

A burning league—leagues, leagues of fire
Arose behind, and ever higher
The flying semi-circle came :
And aye beyond this dreadful pyre
There leapt a man-like thing in flame.

With awful scream doom'd Michael saw
The flying furnace reach Black-Law :
" *Blood, bride, and bier, the auld rune saith*
Hell's wind tae me ae nicht sall blaw,
The nicht I ride unto my death ! "

" *The blood of Stair is round me now :*
My bride can laugh to scorn my vow :
My bier, my bier, ah sall it be
Wi' a crown o' fire around my brow
Or deep within the cauld saut sea ! "

Like lightning, over Black-Law's slope
Michael fled swift with sudden hope :
What though the forest roared behind—
He yet might gain the cliff and grope
For where the sheep-paths twist and wind.

The air was like a furnace-blast
And all the dome of heaven one vast
Expanse of flame and fiery wings :
To the cliff's edge, ere all be past,
With shriek on shriek lost Michael springs.

But none can hear his bitter call,
None, none can see him sway and fall—
Yea, one there is that shrills his name !
" O God, it is my ain lost saul
That I hae girt wi' deathless flame ! "

With waving arms and dreadful cries
He cowers beneath those glaring eyes—
But all in vain—in vain—in vain !
His own soul clasps him as its prize
And scorches death upon his brain.

Body and soul together swing
Adown the night until they fling
The hissing sea-spray far and wide :
At morn the fresh sea-wind will bring
A black corpse tossing on the tide.

THE TWIN-SOUL

In the dead of the night a spirit came :
Her moon-white face and her eyes of flame
Were known to me :—I called her name—
    The name that shall not be spoken at all
    Till Death hath this body of mine in thrall !

And she laughed to see me lying there,
Wrapped in the living-corpse bloody and fair,
And my soul 'mid its thin films shining bare—
    And I rose and followed her glance so
      sweet
    And passed from the house with noiseless
      feet.

I know not myself what I knew, what I saw !
I know that it filled me with trouble and awe,
With pain that still at my heart doth gnaw :
    That she with her wild eyes witched my
      soul
    And whispered the name of the Unknown
      Goal.

The Twin-Soul

O, wild was her laugh, and wild was my cry
When with one long flash and a weary sigh
I awoke as from sleep bewilderingly :
   Her voice, her eyes, they are with me still,
   O Spirit-Enchantress, O Demon-Will !

THE ISLE OF LOST DREAMS

There is an isle beyond our ken,
Haunted by Dreams of weary men.
Grey Hopes enshadow it with wings
Weary with burdens of old things :
There the insatiate water-springs
Rise with the tears of all who weep :
And deep within it, deep, oh deep
The furtive voice of Sorrow sings.
    There evermore,
    Till Time be o'er,
Sad, oh so sad, the Dreams of men
Drift through the isle beyond our ken.

THE DEATH-CHILD

She sits beneath the elder-tree
  And sings her song so sweet,
And dreams o'er the burn that darksomely
  Runs by her moon-white feet.

Her hair is dark as starless night,
  Her flower-crown'd face is pale,
But oh, her eyes are lit with light
  Of dread ancestral bale.

She sings an eerie song, so wild
  With immemorial dule—
Though young and fair Death's mortal child
  That sits by that dark pool.

And oft she cries an eldritch scream
  When red with human blood
The burn becomes a crimson stream,
  A wild, red, surging flood :

Or shrinks, when some swift tide of tears—
  The weeping of the world—
Dark eddying 'neath man's phantom-fears,
  Is o'er the red stream hurl'd.

The Death-Child

For hours beneath the elder-tree
  She broods beside the stream ;
Her dark eyes filled with mystery,
  Her dark soul rapt in dream.

The lapsing flow she heedeth not
  Though deepest depths she scans :
Life is the shade that clouds her thought,
  As Death's the eclipse of man's.

Time seems but as a bitter thing
  Remember'd from of yore :
Yet ah (she thinks) her song she'll sing
  When Time's long reign is o'er.

Erstwhiles she bends alow to hear
  What the swift water sings,
The torrent running darkly clear
  With secrets of all things.

And then she smiles a strange sad smile,
  And lets her harp lie long ;
The death-waves oft may rise the while,
  She greets them with no song.

Few ever cross that dreary moor,
  Few see that flower-crown'd head ;
But whoso knows that wild song's lure
  Knoweth that he is dead.

137

THE COVES OF CRAIL

The moon-white waters wash and leap,
  The dark tide floods the Coves of Crail ;
Sound, sound he lies in dreamless sleep,
  Nor hears the sea-wind wail.

The pale gold of his oozy locks,
  Doth hither drift and thither wave ;
His thin hands plash against the rocks,
  His white lips nothing crave.

Afar away she laughs and sings—
  A song he loved, a wild sea-strain—
Of how the mermen weave their rings
  Upon the reef-set main.

Sound, sound he lies in dreamless sleep,
  Nor hears the sea-wind wail,
Tho' with the tide his white hands creep
  Amid the Coves of Crail.

FROM

SOSPIRI DI ROMA

PRELUDE

Supra un munti sparman stu bellu ciuri!
Chistu è lu ciuri di la tò billizza
Sicilian Canzuno.

In a grove of ilex
Of oak and of chestnut,
Far on the sunswept
Heights of Tusculum,
There groweth a blossom,
A snow-white bloom,
Which many have heard of,
But few have seen.
Oft bright as the morning,
Oft pale as moonlight,
There in the greenness,
In shadow and sunshine
It grows, awaiting
The hand that shall pluck it :
For this blossom springeth
From the heart of a poet
And of her who loved him
In the long ago,
Here on the sunswept

Prelude

Heights of Tusculum.
And them it awaiteth,
Deep lovers only,
Kindred of those
Who loved and passioned
There, and whose heart's-blood
Wrought from the Earth
This marvellous blossom,
The Shadow-Lily,
The Flower of Dream.

Few that shall see it,
Fewer still
Those that shall pluck it :
But whoso gathers
That snow-white blossom
Shall love for ever,
For the passionate breath
Of the Shadow-Lily
Is Deathless Joy :
And whoso plucks it, keeps it, treasures it,
Has sunshine ever
About the heart,
Deep in the heart immortal sunshine :
For this is the gift of the snow-white
    blossom,
This is the gift of the Flower of Dream.

SUSURRO

Breath o' the grass,
Ripple of wandering wind,
Murmur of tremulous leaves :
A moonbeam moving white
Like a ghost across the plain :
A shadow on the road :
And high up, high,
From the cypress-bough,
A long sweet melancholy note.
Silence.
And the topmost spray
Of the cypress-bough is still
As a wavelet in a pool :
The road lies duskily bare :
The plain is a misty gloom :
Still are the tremulous leaves ;
Scarce a last ripple of wind,
Scarce a breath i' the grass.
Hush : the tired wind sleeps :
Is it the wind's breath, or
Breath o' the grass.

HIGH NOON AT MIDSUMMER
ON THE CAMPAGNA

High noon,
And from the purple-veilèd hills
To where Rome lies in azure mist,
Scarce any breath of wind
Upon this vast and solitary waste,
These leagues of sunscorch'd grass
Where i' the dawn the scrambling goats
    maintain
A hardy feast,
And where, when the warm yellow moon-
    light floods the flats,
Gaunt laggard sheep browse spectrally for
    hours
While not less gaunt and spectral shepherds
    stand
Brooding, or with hollow vacant eyes
Stare down the long perspectives of the
    dusk.
Now not a breath :
No sound ;

High Noon at Midsummer on the Campagna

No living thing,
Save where the beetle jars his crackling
    shards,
Or where the hoarse cicala fills
The heavy heated hour with palpitant whirr.
Yet hark !
Comes not a low deep whisper from the
    ground,
A sigh as though the immemorial past
Breathed here a long, slow, breath ?
Hush'd nations sleep below ; lost empires
    here
Are dust ; and deeper still,
Dim shadowy peoples are the mould that
    warms
The roots of every flower that blooms and
    blows :
Even as we, too, bloom and fade,
Who are so fain
To be as the Night that dies not, but forever
Weaves her immortal web of starry fires ;
To be as Time itself,
Time, whose vast holocausts
Lie here, deep buried from the ken of men,
Here, where no breath of wind
Ruffles the brooding heat,
The breathless blazing heat
Of Noon.

THE FOUNTAIN OF THE
ACQUA PAOLA

Not where thy turbid wave
Flowing Maremma-ward,
Moves heavily, Tiber,
Through Rome the Eternal,
Not there her music, not there her joy is :
But where on Janiculum
The tall pines
Sing their high song, with deeper therein,
    like an echo
Heard in a mountain-hollow where cataracts
    break,
A sound as of surge and of foaming :
Yes, there where the echoing pines
Whisper to high wandering winds
The rush and the surge and the splendour
Where the Acqua Paola thunders
Into its fount gigantic,
With noise like a tempest cleaving
With mighty wings
The norland forests.

146

The Fountain of the Acqua Paola

From dayspring, yellow and green
And grey as a swan's breastfeather,
To sunset's amber and gold
And the white star of dusk,
And through the moon-white hours
Till only Hesperus hangs
His quivering tremulous disc
O'er the faint-flushed forehead of Dawn—
All hours, all days, forever
Surgeth the singing flood,
With chant and paean glorious,
With foam and splash and splendour,
A music wild, barbaric,
That calleth loud over Rome,
Laughing, mocking, rejoicing :
The sound of the waves when Ocean
Laughs at the vanishing land
And, fronting her shoreless leagues,
Remembers the ruined empires
That now are the drift and shingle
In cavernous hollows under
Her zone of Oblivion,
Silence that nought shall break,
Eternal calm.

Foam, spray and splendour
Of rushing waters,
Grey-blue as the pale blue dome
That circleth the morning star

While still his fires are brighter
Than the wanwhite fire of the moon.
Foam, spray, and surge
Of rushing waters !
O the hot flood of sunshine
Yellowly pouring
Over and into thee, jubilant Fountain :
Thy cataracts filled
With vanishing rainbows,
Shimmering lights
As though the Aurora's
Wild polar fires
Flashed in thy happy bubbles, died in thy
    foam.

Ever in joyous laughter
Thy wavelets are dancing,
Little waves with crests bright with sun-
    light
Tossing their foamy arms,
Laughing and leaping,
Whirling, inweaving,
Rippling at last and sleepily laving
The mossed stone-barriers
That clasp them round.
Bright too and joyous,
They, in the moonshine,
When the falling waters
Are as wreaths of snow

The Fountain of the Acqua Paola

Falling for ever
Down mountain-flanks,
Like melting snows
In the high hill-hollows
Seen from the valleys
And seeming to fall,
To fall forever
A flower of water,
Silent, and stirred not
By any wind.

Bright too and joyous
In darkling nights,
When the moon shroudeth
Her face in a veil
Of cloudy vapours,
Or, like a flower
I' the wane of its beauty,
Droopeth and falleth
Till lost to sight,
Stoopeth and fadeth
Into the dark—
Or when like a sickle
Thin and silvern
She moveth slowly
Through the starry fields,
Moveth slowly
'Mid the flowers of the stars
In the harvest-fields

Of Eternity :
Bright too and joyous,
For then the shadows
Play with the foam-lights,
With the flying whiteness,
And snowy surging.
But brighter, more joyous,
Save when the moon-flower
In all her splendour
Floats on thy bosom,
Or, rather, dreameth
Deep in the heart of thee
O happy Fountain :
Brighter, more joyous,
Thee, when amidst thee,
Strewn through thy waters,
The stars are sown
As seed multitudinous,
As silvern seed
In thy shadowy-furrows :
Seed of the skiey flowers
That in the heavens
Bloom forever,
Blossoms and blooms of
Eternal splendour.
Then is thy joy most,
O jubilant Fountain,
Then are thy waters
Sweetest of song,

The Fountain of the Acqua Paola

Then do thy waters
Surge, leap, rejoicing,
Lave, and lapse slowly
To haunted stillness
And darkling dreams :
Then is thy music rarest,
Wildest and sweetest
Music of Rome—
Rome the Eternal,
Through whose heart of shadow
Moveth slowly
Flowing Maremma-ward
Thy murmur, Tiber,
Thy muffled voice,
Whom none interpreteth
But boding, ominous,
Is as the sound of
Murmurous seas
Heard afar inland—
There, where Maremma-ward
Flowing heavily,
Moveth, Tiber,
Thy turbid wave.

CLOUDS

(*Agro Romano*)

As though the dead cities
Of the ancient time
Were builded again
In the heights of heaven,
With spires of amber
And golden domes,
Wide streets of topaz and amethyst ways ;
Far o'er the pale blue waste,
Oft purple-shadowed,
Of the Agro Romano,
Rises the splendid
City of Cloud.
There must the winds be soft as the twilight
Invisibly falling when the day-star has
    wester'd ;
There must the rainbows trail up through
    the sunlight,
So fair are the hues on those white snowy
    masses.
Mountainous glories,

Clouds

They move superbly ;
Crumbling so slowly,
That none perceives when
The golden domes
Are sunk in the valleys
Of fathomless snow,
Or when, in silence,
The loftiest spires
Fade into smoke, or as vapour that passeth
When the hot breath of noon
Thirsts through the firmament.
Beautiful, beautiful,
The City of Cloud,
In splendour ruinous,
With golden domes,
And spires of amber,
Builded superbly
In the heights of heaven.

RED POPPIES

(In the Sabine valleys near Rome)

Through the seeding grass,
And the tall corn,
The wind goes :
With nimble feet,
And blithe voice,
Calling, calling,
The wind goes
Through the seeding grass,
And the tall corn.

What calleth the wind,
Passing by—
The shepherd-wind ?
Far and near
He laugheth low
And the red poppies
Lift their heads
And toss i' the sun.
A thousand thousand blooms
Tost i' the air,

154

Red Poppies

Banners of joy,
For 'tis the shepherd-wind
Passing by,
Singing and laughing low
Through the seeding grass
And the tall corn.

THE WHITE PEACOCK

Here where the sunlight
Floodeth the garden,
Where the pomegranate
Reareth its glory
Of gorgeous blossom ;
Where the oleanders
Dream through the noontides ;
And, like surf o' the sea
Round cliffs of basalt,
The thick magnolias
In billowy masses
Front the sombre green of the ilexes :
Here where the heat lies
Pale blue in the hollows,
Where blue are the shadows
On the fronds of the cactus,
Where pale blue the gleaming
Of fir and cypress,
With the cones upon them
Amber or glowing
With virgin gold :

The White Peacock

Here where the honey-flower
Makes the heat fragrant,
As though from the gardens
Of Gulistan,
Where the bulbul singeth
Through a mist of roses
A breath were borne :
Here where the dream-flowers,
The cream-white poppies
Silently waver,
And where the Scirocco,
Faint in the hollows,
Foldeth his soft white wings in the sunlight,
And lieth sleeping
Deep in the heart of
A sea of white violets :
Here, as the breath, as the soul of this
    beauty
Moveth in silence, and dreamlike, and slowly,
White as a snow-drift in mountain-valleys
When softly upon it the gold light lingers :
White as the foam o' the sea that is driven
O'er billows of azure agleam with sun-
    yellow :
Cream-white and soft as the breasts of a girl,
Moves the White Peacock, as though
    through the noontide
A dream of the moonlight were real for a
    moment.

Dim on the beautiful fan that he spreadeth,
Foldeth and spreadeth abroad in the sun-
    light,
Dim on the cream-white are blue adum-
    brations,
Shadows so pale in their delicate blueness
That visions they seem as of vanishing
    violets,
The fragrant white violets veined with
    azure,
Pale, pale as the breath of blue smoke in far
    woodlands.
Here, as the breath, as the soul of this
    beauty,
White as a cloud through the heats of the
    noontide
Moves the White Peacock.

THE SWIMMER OF NEMI

(The Lake of Nemi : September)

White through the azure,
The purple blueness,
Of Nemi's waters
The swimmer goeth.
Ivory-white, or wan white as roses
Yellowed and tanned by the suns of the
    Orient,
His strong limbs sever the violet hollows ;
A shimmer of white fantastic motions
Wavering deep through the lake as he
    swimmeth.
Like gorse in the sunlight the gold of his
    yellow hair,
Yellow with sunshine and bright as with
    dew-drops,
Spray of the waters flung back as he tosseth
His head i' the sunlight in the midst of his
    laughter :
Red o'er his body, blossom-white 'mid the
    blueness,

And trailing behind him in glory of scarlet,
A branch of the red-berried ash of the
    mountains.
White as a moonbeam
Drifting athwart
The purple twilight,
The swimmer goeth—
Joyously laughing,
With o'er his shoulders,
Agleam in the sunshine
The trailing branch
With the scarlet berries.
Green are the leaves, and scarlet the berries,
White are the limbs of the swimmer beyond
    them,
Blue the deep heart of the still, brooding
    lakelet,
Pale-blue the hills in the haze of September,
The high Alban hills in their silence and
    beauty,
Purple the depths of the windless heaven
Curv'd like a flower o'er the waters of Nemi.

AL FAR DELLA NOTTE

Hark !
As a bubbling fount
That suddenly wells
And rises in tall spiral waves and flying
    spray,
The high, sweet, quavering, throbbing voice
Of the nightingale !
Not yet the purple veil of dusk has fallen,
But o'er the yellow band
That binds the west
The vesper star beats like the pulse of
    heaven.

Up from the fields
The peasants troop
Singing their songs of love :
And oft the twang of thin string'd music
    breaks
High o'er the welcoming shouts,
The homing laughter.
The whirling bats are out,
And to and fro

Al Far della Notte

The blue swifts wheel
Where, i' the shallows of the dusk,
The grey moths flutter
Over the pale blooms
Of the night-flowering bay.
Softly adown the slopes,
And o'er the plain,
Ave Maria
Solemnly soundeth.
The long day is over.
Dusk, and silence now :
And Night, that is as dew
On the Flower of the World.

THISTLEDOWN

(Spring on the Campagna)

Bloweth like snow
From the grey thistles
The thistledown :
And the fairy-feathers
O' the dandelion
Are tossed by the breeze
Hither and thither :
Over the grasses,
The seeding grasses
Where the poppies shake
And the campions waver,
And where the clover,
Purple and white,
Fills leagues with the fragrance
Of sunsweet honey ;
Hither and thither
The fairy-feathers
O' the dandelion,
And white puff-balls
O' the thistledown,
Merrily dancing,
Light on the breeze,

Thistledown

Wheeling and sailing;
And laughing to scorn
The butterflies
And the moths of azure ;
Blowing like snow
Or foam o' the sea,
Hither and thither
Upward and downward.

Now for a moment
A thistledown
On a white ball resteth,
Sunbleached and hollow ;
A human skull
Of the ancient days,
When Sabines and Latins
Made all the land here
As red with blood
As it now is scarlet
With flaming poppies.
Now the feathers,
O' the dandelion,
Like sunlit swan's-down
Long tost by the wind
O'er the laughter of waters,
Are blown like surf
On a hidden rock—
A broken arch
Of a Roman temple,

164

Thistledown

Where long, long ago,
The swarthy priests
Worshipped their Gods,
The Gods now less than
The very dust
Whence the green grass springeth !
But for a moment, then the wind takes
    them,
Blows them, plays with them,
Tosses them high through the gold of the
    sunshine,
Wavers them upward, wavers them down-
    ward.
Hither and thither among the white butter-
    flies,
Over and under the blue-moths and honey-
    bees,
Over the leagues of blossoming clover,
Purple and white, the sweet-smelling clover,
Far o'er the grasses,
And grey hanging thistles,
Hither and thither
Are floating and sailing
The fairy-feathers
O' the dandelion,
Bloweth like snow
The joy o' the meadows,
The thistledown.

THE SHEPHERD

(Near the Theatre of Marcellus :
Piazza Montanara)

Solitary he stands,
Clad in his goat-skins,
Though all about him
The busy throng
Cometh and goeth.
Overhead, the vast ruin,
Wind-worn, time-wrought,
Gloomily rises.
Scarce doth he note it,
Yet doth it give him
The touch of nearness,
Which the soul craves for
In alien places :
As the strayed mariner,
Yearning, far inland,
For sight of the sea,
Smiles when he fingers a rope, or
Heareth the wind
Surge round the hedgerows

The Shepherd

As erst through the cordage ;
Or, on the endless, dusty, white high-road
Puts his ear to the pole
Vibrating with song, as the mast
Erewhile rang with the hum
Of the hurricane.

What doth he here,
Away from the pastures
On the desolate Campagna ?
From his haggard face
Sorrowfully his wild black eyes
Stare on the weariness,
The noise, and hurry,
And surge of the traffic.
Sometimes, a faint smile
Flitteth athwart his face,
When a woman, from the well,
Passeth by with a conca
Poised on her head :
Thus oft hath he seen
The peasant girls
In the little hamlets
Far out on the plain :
Or when a wine-cart
With its tall cappoto
A-swing like a high tent windswayed sidewise,
Rattles in from the Appian highway,
White with the dust of the Alban hills.

The Shepherd

What doth he here,
He in whose eyes are
The passion of the desert :
He in whose ears rings
The free music
Of the winds that wander
Through the desert-ruins ?
Not here, O Shepherd,
Wouldst thou fain dwell,
Though in the Holy City
God's Regent lives :
Better the desolate waste,
Better the free lone life,
For there thou canst breathe,
There silence abideth,
There, not the Regent,
But God himself
Dwelleth and speaketh.

THE MANDOLIN

Tinkle-trink,   tinkle-trink,   trinkle-trinkle,
  trink !
Hark, the mandolin !
Through the dusk the merry music falleth
  sweet.
Where the fountain falls,
Where the fountain falls all shimmering in
  the moonshine white,
Tinkle-trink,   tinkle-trink,   trinkle-trinkle,
  trink !
Where the wind-stirred olives quiver,
Quiver, quiver, leaves a-quiver,
White as silver in the moonlight but like
  bat-wings in the dusk,
Where the great grey moths sail slowly
Slowly, slowly, like faint dreams
In the wildering woods of Sleep,
Where no night or day is,
But only, in dim twilights, the wan sheen
Of the Moon of Sleep.

Hark, the mandolin !
Where the dark-coned cypress rises,

The Mandolin

Thin, more thin, till threadlike, wavering
The last spray soars up as smoke,
As a vanishing breath of incense,
To the silent stars that glimmer
In the veil of purple darkness,
The deep vault of heaven that seemeth
As a veil that falleth,
A dark veil that foldeth gently
The tired day-worn world, breathing stilly
    as a sleeping child.
Hark, the mandolin :
And a soft low sound of laughter !
Tinkle-trink,   tinkle-trink,   trinkle-trinkle,
    trink !

Hush : from out the cypress standing
Black against the yellow moonlight
What a thrill, what a sob, what a sudden
    rapture flung
Athwart the dark !
Passion of song !
Silence again, save 'mid the whispering
    leaves
The unquiet wind, that as the tide
Cometh and goeth.
Now one long thrilling note, prolonged and
    sweet,
And then a low swift stir,
A whirr of fluttering wings,

The Mandolin

And, in the laurels near, two nested nightin-
      gales !
Loud, loud, the mandolin,
Tinkle-trink,   tinkle-trink,   trinkle-trinkle,
      trink,
Trink, trink, trinkle-trink !
Through the fragrant silent night it draweth
      near,
Ah, the low cry, the little laugh, the rustle :
Tinkle-trink—hush,   a   kiss—*tinkle-trink*—
      hush—hush—
Tinkle-trink,   tinkle-trink,   trinkle-trinkle,
      trink !

Where the shadows massed together
Make a hollow darkness, girt
By the yellow flood of moonshine floating
      by,
Where the groves of ilex whisper
In the silence, fragrant, sweet,
Where the ilexes are dreaming
In their depths of darkest shadow,
Move the fireflies slowly,
Mazily inweaving,
Interweaving, interflowing ;
Wandering fires, like little lanterns
Borne by souls of birds and flowers
Seeking ever resurrection
In the gladsome world of sunshine ;
      171

The Mandolin

Seekly vainly through the darkness
In beneath the ilex-branches
Where the very moonshine faileth,
And the dark grey moths wave wanly
Flitting from the outer gloaming.
Oh, the fragrance, and the mystery, and the
    silence !
Where the fireflies, 'mid the ilex,
Rise and fall, recross, inweave
In an endless wavy motion,
In a slow aerial dancing
In a maze of little flames
In and out the ilex-branches :
Hush ! the mandolin !
Louder still, and louder, louder :
Ah, the happy laugh, and rustle,
Rustle, rustle,
Ah, the kiss, the cry, the rapture.
Silence, where the ilex-branches
Loom out faintly from their darkness
Where, slow-wandering flames, the fireflies
Rise and fall, recross, inweave
In an endless wavy motion,
In a slow aerial dancing.

Silence : not a breath is stirring :
Not a leaflet quivers faintly.
Silence : even the bats are silent
Wheeling swiftly through the upper air,

The Mandolin

Where the gnat's thin shrilling music
Fades into the flooding moonlight :
Hush, low whispered words and kisses,
Hush, a cry of pain, of rapture.
Not a sound, a sound thereafter,
But a low sweet sigh of breathing,
And, from out the flowering laurel,
Just a twittering breath of music,
Just a long-drawn pulsing note
Of a sweet and passionate answer.
Silence : hark, a stir—low laughter—
Whispered words—and rustle—rustle—
Trink—trink—the mandolin !
Hark, it trinkles down the valley,
Trink-trink, trinkle-trink, trinkle-trink !
Past the cistus, blooming whitely,
Past the oleander-bushes,
Past the ilexes and olives,
Where the two tall pines are whispering
With the sleepy wind that foldeth
His tired pinions ere he sleepeth
On the flood of amber moonlight.
Wind o' the night, tired wind o' night—
Tinkle-trink, trink, trinkle-trink,
Trink, trinkle-trink,
Trink !

BAT-WINGS

Flitter, flitter, through the twilight,
Pipistrello :
Where the moonshine glitters
Waver thy swart wings,
Darting hither, thither,
Swift as wheeling swallow.
Where the shadows gather
In and out thou flittest,
Flitter, flitter,
Waver, waver,
Pipistrello.
Thin thy faint aerial song is,
Thin and fainter than the shrilling
Of the gnats thou chasest wildly,
But how delicately dainty—
Thin and faint and wavering also,
In the high sweet upper air,
Where the gnats weave endless mazes
In their pyramidal dances—
And thy dusky wings go flutter,
Flutter, flutter,
Waver, waver,
But without a sound or rustle
Through the purple air of twilight.
Flitter, flitter, flutter, flitter,
Pipistrello.

174

LA VELIA

(The Sea-Gull : Pontine Marshes)

Here where the marsh
Waves white with ranunculus,
Where the yellow daffodil
Flieth his banner
In the fetid air,
And oft 'mid the bulrushes
Rustleth the porcupine
Or surgeth the boar—
Though bloweth rarely
The fresh wind,
The Tramontana,
And only Scirocco
Heavily lifts
The feathery plumes the tall canes carry :
What dost thou here,
O bird of the ocean ?
Here, where the marshes
Are never stirred
By the pulse of the tides ;
Here where the white mists

Crawl on the swamp,
But never the rush and the surge of the
　　billows ?
White as a snowflake thou gleamest, and
　　passest :
Drearier now the chill waste of the Stagno,
Wearier now the dull silence and boding.
Would that again
Thy glad presence were gleaming
Here where the marsh
Steams white in the sunshine ;
For swift on my sight,
As thy white wings wavered,
Broke the sea in its beauty,
With foam, and splendour
Of rolling waves :
And loud on my ears (O the longing, the
　　yearning)
When thy cry filled the silence,
Came the surge of the sea
And the tumult of waters.

SPUMA DAL MARE

(On the Latin Coast)

Flower o' the wave,
White foam of the waters,
The many-coloured :
Here blue as a hare-bell,
Here pale as the turquoise ;
Here green as the grasses
Of mountain hollows,
Here lucent as jade when wet in the sun-
    shine,
Here paler than apples ere ruddied by
    autumn.
Depths o' the purple !
Amethyst yonder,
Yonder as ling on the hills of October,
With shadows as deep,
Where islets of sea-wrack
Wave in the shallows,
As the sheen of the feathers
On the blue-green breast
Of the bird of the Orient,
The splendid peacock.

Spuma dal Mare

Foam o' the waves,
White crests ashine
With a dazzle of sunlight !
Here the low breakers are rolling through
    shallows,
Yellow and muddied, the hue of the topaz
Ere cut from the boulder ;
Save when the sunlight swims through them
    slantwise,
When inward they roll
Long billows of amber,
Crowned with pale yellow
And grey-green spume.
Here wan grey their slopes
Where the broken lights reach them,
Dull grey of pearl, and dappled, and
    darkling,
As when 'mid the high
Northward drift of the clouds,
Scirocco bloweth
With soft fanning breath.

Foam o' the waves,
Blown blossoms of ocean,
White flowers of the waters,
The many-coloured.

THE BATHER

Where the sea-wind ruffles
The pale pink blooms
Of the fragrant Daphne,
And passeth softly
Over the sward
Of the cyclamen-blossoms,
The Bather stands.
Rosy white, as a cloud at the dawning,
Silent she stands,
And looks far seaward,
As a seabird, dreaming
On some lone rock,
Poiseth his pinions
Ere over the waters
He moves like a vision
On motionless wings.

Beautiful, beautiful,
The sunlit gleam
Of her naked body,
Ivory-white 'mid the cyclamen-blossoms

The Bather

A wave o' the sea 'mid the blooms of the
    Daphne.
Blue as the innermost heart of the ocean
The arch of the sky where the wood runneth
    seaward,
Blue as the depths of the innermost heaven
The vast heaving breast of the slow-moving
    waters :
Green the thick grasses that run from the
    woodland,
Green as the heart of the foam-crested
    billows
Curving a moment ere washing far inland
Up the long reach of the sands gleaming
    golden.
The land-breath beareth
Afar the fragrance
Of thyme and basil
And clustered rosemary ;
And o'er the fennel,
And through the broom,
It floateth softly,
As the wind of noon
That cometh and goeth
Though none hearkens
Its downy wings.
And keen, the seawind
Bears up the odours
Of blossoming pinks

The Bather

And salt rock-grasses,
Of rustling seaweed
And mosses of pools
Where the rosy blooms
Of the sea-flowers open
'Mid stranded waves.
As a water-lily
Touched by the breath
Of sunrise-glory,
Moveth and swayeth
With tremulous joy,
So o'er the sunlit
White gleaming body
Of the beautiful bather
Passeth a quiver
Rosy-white, as a cloud at the dawning,
Poised like a swallow that meeteth the wind,
For a moment she standeth
Where the sea-wind softly
Moveth over
The thick pink sward of the cyclamen-
    blossoms.
Moveth and rustleth
With faint susurrus
The pale pink blooms
Of the fragrant Daphne.

THE WILD MARE

Like a breath that comes and goes
O'er the waveless waste
Of sleeping Ocean,
So sweeps across the plain
The herd of wild horses.
Like banners in the wind
Their flying tails,
Their streaming manes :
And like spume of the sea
Fang'd by breakers,
The white froth tossed from their blood-red
    nostrils.
Out from the midst of them
Dasheth a white mare,
White as a swan in the pride of her beauty :
And, like the whirlwind,
Following after,
A snorting stallion,
Swart as an Indian
Diver of coral !
Wild the gyrations,
The rush and the whirl ;

The Wild Mare

Loud the hot panting
Of the snow-white mare,
As swift upon her
The stallion gaineth :
Fierce the proud snorting
Of him, victorious :
And loud, swelling loud on the wind from
    the mountains,
The hoarse savage tumult of neighing and
    stamping
Where, wheeling, the herd of wild horses
    awaiteth—
Ears thrown back, tails thrashing their
    flanks or swept under—
The challenging scream of the conqueror-
    stallion.

SCIROCCO

(*June*)

Softly as feathers
That fall through the twilight
When wild swans are winging
Back to the northward :
Softly as waters,
Unruffled, and tideless,
Laving the mosses
Of inland seas :
Soft through the forest,
And down through the valley,
Light as a breath o'er the pools of the
    marish,
Still as a moonbeam over the pastures, .
Goeth Scirocco.

Warm his breath :
The night-flowers know it,
Love it, and open
Their blooms for its sweetness :
Warm the tender low wind of his pinions

184

Scirocco

Scarce brushing together the spires of the
    grasses :
Ah, how they whisper, the little green leaflets
Black in the dusk or grey in the moonlight :
Ah, how they whisper and shiver, the
    tremulous
Leaves of the poplar, and shimmer and rustle
When soft as a vapour that steals from the
    marshes
The wings of Scirocco fan silently through
    them.

Oft-times he lingers
By ruined nests
Deep in the hedgerows,
And bloweth a feather
In little eddies,
A yellow feather
That once had fluttered
On a breast alive with
A rapture of song :
But slowly ceaseth,
And passeth sadly.
Oft-times he riseth
Up through the branches
Where the fireflies wander
Up through the branches
Of oak and chestnut,
And stirs so gently

Scirocco

With sway of his wings
That the leaves, dreaming,
Think that a moonbeam
Only, or moonshine,
Moves through the heart of them.
Upward he soareth
Oft, silently floating
Through the purple æther,
Still as the fern-owl over the covert,
Or as allocco haunting the woodland,
Up to the soft curded foam of the cloudlets,
The white dappled cloudlets the south-
    wind bringeth.
There, dreaming, he moveth
Or sails through the moonlight,
Till chill in the high upper air and the
    silence,
Slowly he sinketh
Earthward again,
Silently floateth
Down o'er the woodlands :
Foldeth his wings and slow through the
    branches
Drifts, scarcely breathing,
Till tired, 'mid the flowers or the hedgerows
    he creepeth,
Whispers alow 'mid the spires of the grasses,
Or swooning at last to motionless slumber
Floats like a shadow adrift on the pastures.

THE WIND AT FIDENAE

Fresh from the Sabines,
The Beautiful Hills,
The wind bloweth.
Down o'er the slopes,
Where the olives whiten
As though the feet
Of the wind were snow-clad :
Out o'er the plain
Where a paradise
Of wild blooms waveth,
And where, in the sunswept
Leagues of azure,
A thousand larks are
As a thousand founts
'Mid the perfect joy of
The depth of heaven.
Swift o'er the heights,
And over the valleys
Where the grey oxen sleepily stand,
Down, like a wild hawk swooping earthward,
Over the winding reaches of Tiber,
Bloweth the wind !

The Wind at Fidenae

How the wind bloweth,
Here on the steeps of
Ancient Fidenae,
Where no voice soundeth
Now, save the shepherd
Calling his sheep ;
And where none wander
But only the cloud-shadows,
Vague ghosts of the past.
Sweet and fresh from the Sabines,
Now as of yore,
When Etruscan maidens
Laughed as their lovers
Mocked the damsels
Of alien Rome,
Sweet with the same young breath o' the
    world
Bloweth the wind.

SORGENDO DA LUNA

No sound,
Save the hush'd breath,
The slowly flowing, 刻 ⼘
The long and low withdrawing breath of
    Rome.
Not a leaf quivers, where the dark,
With eyes of rayless shadow and moonlit
    hair,
Dreams in the black
And hollow cavernous depth of the ilex-
    trees.
No sound,
Save the hush'd breath of Rome,
And sweet and fresh and clear
The bubbling, swaying, ever quavering jet
Of water fill'd with pale nocturnal gleams,
That, in the broad low fount,
Falleth,
Falleth and riseth,
Riseth and falleth, swayeth and surgeth,
    ever
A spring of life and joy where ceaselessly

Sorgendo da Luna

The shadow of two sovran powers make
A terror without fear, a night that hath no
　　dark,
Time, with his sunlit wings,
Death, with his pinions vast and duskily
　　dim :
Time, breathing vanishing life :
Death, breathing low
From twilights of Oblivion whence Time
　　rose
A wild and wandering star forlornly whirled,
Seen for a moment, ere for ever lost.
Up from the marble fount
The water leaps,
Sways in the moonshine, springeth,
　　springeth,
Falleth and riseth,
Like sweet faint lapping music,
Soft gurgling notes of woodland brooks that
　　wander
Low laughing where the hollowed stones are
　　green
With slippery moss that hath a trickling
　　sound :
Leapeth and springeth,
Singing forever
A wayward song.
While the vast wings of Time and Death
　　drift slowly,

Sorgendo da Luna

While, faint and far, the tides of life
Sigh in a long scarce audible breath from
    Rome,
Or faintlier still withdraw down shores of
    dusk ;
For ever singing
It leapeth and falleth :
Falleth and leapeth,
Falleth,
And falleth.

IN JULY

(South of Rome)

Pale-rose the dust lying thick upon the
    road :
Grey-green the thirsty grasses by the way.
The long flat silvery sheen of the vast
    champaign
Shimmers beneath the blazing tide of noon.
The blood-red poppies flame
Like furnace-breaths :
Like wan vague dreams the misty lavender
Drifts greyly through the quivering maze;
    or seems
Thus through the visionary glow to drift.
On the far slope, beyond the ruin'd arch,
A grey-white cloudlet rests,
The cluster'd sheep alow : close, moveless
    all,
And silent, save when faintly from their
    midst
A slumberous tinkle comes,
Cometh, and goeth.

In July

Low-stretch'd in the blue shade,
Beneath the ruin
The shepherd sleeps.
Nought stirs.
The wind moves not, nor with the faintest
    breath
Toucheth the half-fallen blooms of the
    asphodels.
Here only, where the pale pink ash
Of the long road doth slowly flush to rose,
A bronze-wing'd beetle moveth low,
And sends one tiny puff of smoke-like dust
Faint through the golden glimmer of the
    heat.

A DREAM AT ARDEA

(*Maremma*)

Where Ardea, the cliff-girt,
Looks to the Sea,
Dreaming forever
In her desert place
Of her vanished glory—
There too in the tall grass,
Starred with narcissus
And the flaming poppy,
I dreamed a dream.

Not of the days when
The fierce trumpeting
Of the Asian elephants
Made the wild horses
Snort in new terror,
Snort and wheel wildly,
Till o'er the Campagna
They passed like a trail
Of vanishing smoke.
No, nor when

A Dream at Ardea

The brazen clarions
Of the Roman legion
Summoned the hill-folk
To the Punic War :
Nor yet when the shadow
Of the falling star
Of the House of Tarquin
Swept unseen o'er the banquet,
And none, foreseeing,
Drew forth the pure sword
For the foul heart of Sextus.
Nor yet of the ancient days
When the fierce Rutuli
Laughed at the boasting of
The seven-hilled city,
And when on rude altars
White victims lay,
To appease the anger
Of barbarian Gods—
Nay, not of these, not even the far-off,
The ancient time, when the mother of
    Perseus,
Danaë the beautiful, came hither and
    builded
Close to the sea the hill-town which standeth
Now amid leagues of the inland grasses,
White with the surf of the blossoming
    asphodels—
Nay, but only

Of the shrine of her,
Venus, the Beautiful One,
The Well-Beloved.
Lost, it lieth
Deep 'mid the tangle,
Deep 'neath the roots of the flowers and the
    grasses
Drawn like a veil o'er
The face of Maremma.
Only the brown lark
Singing above it,
Only the grey hare
Beneath the wild olive,
Only the linnet aflit in the myrtle,
Only the spotted snake
Writhing swiftly
O'er the thyme and the spikenard,
Only the falcon
Dusking a moment the gold of the yellow
    broom,
Only the things of the air and the desert,
Know where deep in the maze of the under-
    growth
Lieth the shrine of the sacred Goddess,
The shrine of Venus.
Up through the dark blue mist of the hare-
    bells—
All the wild glory, with trailing convolvulus,
Lenten lilies asway in the sunlight,

Wine-dark   anemones,   pasque-flowers   of
    ruby,
Iris and daffodil and sweet-smelling violet,
And   high   over   all   the   white   and   gold
    shining
Where   the   wind   raced   o'er   the   asphodel
    meadows :
All the flower-glory of Spring in Maremma.
But here, just here, a mist of the harebells—
Up through the dark blue mist of the hare-
    bells
Rose like a white smoke hovering gently
Over the windless woodlands of Ostia
Where   the   charcoal-burners   wander   like
    shadows,
Rose a white vapour, stealthily, slowly.

Ah,   but   the   wonder !   the   wan   ghost   of
    Venus
Rose slowly before me :
Dark, deep, and awful the eyes of the vision,
Sad   beyond   words   that   wraith   of   dead
    beauty,
Chill now and solemn
Austere as the grave,
The face that had blanched
The high gods of old,
The face that had led
The heroes of men

From the heights of Caucasus
To the uttermost ends
Of Earth, as leadeth nightly
The Moon, her cohorts
Of perishing billows.
" I am she whom thou lovest : "
" *Nay, whom I worship, Goddess and Queen !* "
" I am she whom thou worshippest : "
" *For thou art Beauty, and Beauty I worship,*
And thou art Love, and Love—"
" Love is Beauty. They love not nor
worship,
They who dissever the one from the
other."
" *Hearken, O Goddess !* "
" Nay, shadow of shadows, why callest me
Goddess !
Far from thy world ' the Goddess ' is
banished.
Ye have chosen the dark : the dark be
with you !
Ye have chosen sorrow : and sorrow is
yours :
O fools that worship vain Gods, and know not
That life is the breath but of perishing dust—
They only live in whose hearts there hath
fallen
The breath of my passion—"
" *O Goddess, fade not !* "

198

" I pass, and behold,
With my passing goeth
The joy of the world ! "

Darkly austere
The face of the Goddess.
Then like a flame
That groweth wan
And flickereth forth from the reach of vision,
The face of Venus
Was seen no more,
Though through the mist
Her eyes gleamed darkly,
Great fires of joy—
Of joy disherited,
But glorious ever
In their lordly scorn,
Their high disdain.

Not till the purple-hued
Wings of the twilight
Waved softly downward
From the Alban hills,
And moved stilly
Over the vast dim leagues of Maremma,
Turned I backward
My wandering steps.
Far o'er the white-glimmering
Breast of the Tyrrhene Sea
(Laid as in sleep at the feet of the hills)

A Dream at Ardea

Rose, dropping liquid fires
Into the wine-dark vault of the heaven,
The Star of Evening,
Venus, the Evening Star :
Eternal, serene,
In deathless beauty
Revolving ever
Through the stellar spheres !

High o'er the shadowy heights
Of the Volscian summits
The full moon soared :
Soared slowly upward
Like a golden nenuphar
In a vaster Nilus
Than that which floweth
Through the heart of Egypt.
The moon that maketh
The world so beautiful,
That moveth so tenderly
Over desolate things,
The moon that giveth
The amber light,
Wherein best blossom
The mystic flowers
Of human love.

Through the darkness
Whelming the waste,
And, like a stealthy tide

A Dream at Ardea

Rising around
Ardea, the cliff-girt,
Wavered the sound of joyous laughter.
Sweet words and sweeter
Fell where the lentisc
Bloomed, and the rosemary :
Loving caresses
Lost in a rustle
Where the hawthorn-bushes
Loomed large in the twilight
Of the fireflies' lanterns.

Deep in the heart of
A myrtle-thicket
A nightingale stirred :
With low sweet note,
Thrilling strangely,
And as though moving
With the breath of its passion
The midmost leaves.
But once her plaint :—
Then wild and glad,
In a free ecstasy,
In utter bliss,
In one high whirl of rapture, sang
His answering song
Her mate, low swaying upon a bough,
With throat full-strained, and quivering wings
Beating with tremulous whirr.

Then I was glad,
For surely I knew
I had dreamed a dream 'neath the spell of
    Maremma.
Not sunk in the drift
Of antique dust,
Lost from the ken of Earth
Within her shrine,
Venus, the Beautiful,
The Queen of Love !
But though no longer
Beheld of man,
Still living and breathing
Through the heart of the world—
Whether in the song,
Passionate, beautiful,
Of the nightingale ;
Or in the glad rapture
Of lovers meeting,
With soft caresses
Hid in the dusk ;
In the fair flower of the vast field of heaven ;
Or in the glow,
The pulsing splendour,
Of the white star of joy,
The Star of Eve.

DE PROFUNDIS

Whence hast thou gone,
O vision belovèd ?
There is silence now
In thy groves, and never
A voice proclaimeth
Thy glory come,
Thy joy rearisen !

O passion of beauty,
Forsake not thus
Those who have worshipped thee,
Body and soul !
Come to us, come to us,
Inviolate, Beautiful,
Thou whose breath
Is as Spring o'er the world,
Whose smile is the flowering
Of the wide green Earth !
Deep in the heart of thee,
Like a moonbeam moving
Through the heart of a hill-lake
Moveth Compassion :

De Profundis

O Belovèd,
Be with us ever,
Thou, the Beautiful,
Passion of Beauty,
Alma Victrix !

ULTIMO SOSPIRO

O dolce primavera pien' di olezzo e amor!
Che fai tu . . . che fai fra tanti fior ?

Colgo le rose amabili dei più soavi odori ;
Colgo le rose affabili e i lunghi gelsomini,
Nei olenti miei giardini io vi tengo al cor.

Roman Folksong.

Joy of the world,
O flower-crown'd Spring,
With thine odorous breath and thy heart of
    love,
Breathe through this verse thy sweet mes-
    sage of longing.
Lo, in the gardens of Alma, whose lovers
Die gladly in worship, but fail not ever,
Oft have I strayed,
Oft have I lingered
When high through the noon the lost lark
    has been singing,
Or when in the moonlight
Soft through the silence has whispered the
    ocean,
Or when, in the dark

Of the ilex-woods,
Where the fireflies wavered
Frail wandering stars,
Not a sound has been heard
But Scirocco rustling
The midmost leaves
Of the trees where he sleepeth.

Roses of love,
White lilies of dream,
Frail blooms that have blossom'd
Into life with thy breathing :
Blow them, O wind,
West wind of the Spring,
Lift them and take them where gardens
    await them,
Lift them and take them to those who
    hearken,
Facing the dawn, for the sounds of the
    morning,
With wide eyes glad with the beautiful
    vision,
O whispers of joy,
O breaths of passion,
O sighs of longing.

EPILOGUE

Il Bosco Sacro

Ah, the sweet silence :
Not a breath stirreth :
Scarce a leaf moveth.

The Dusk, as a dream,
Steals slowly, slowly,
With shadowy feet
Under the branches
Here, in the woodland,
Hushfully seeking
The Night, her lover.

Sweet are the odours
Breath'd through the twilight,
Lovely spirits
Of lovely things.
One by one
Forth-shimmer white stars
Beyond the skiey
Boughs of chestnuts,

Epilogu

Pale Phosphorescence
Gleaming and glancing
As in the wake
Of a windspent vessel
That, moonlike, drifts
With motionless motion.

Peace : utter peace.
Not a sound riseth
From where in the hollow
The town lies dreaming :
Not a cry from the pastures
That far below
Are drowsed in the shadows.
Only afar,
On the dim Campagna,
Peace, utter peace :
On the pastures, peace
Low in the hollows,
Deep in the woodlands,
High on the hill-slopes,
Rest, utter rest,
Utter peace.

Suddenly . . . thrilling
Long-drawn vibrations !
Passionate preludes
Of passionate song
O the wild music

Epilogue

Tost through the silence,
As a swaying fountain
Is swept by the wind's wings
Far through the sunshine,
A mist of flashing
And falling spray.
How the hush of the stillness
Deepeneth slowly. . . .
Till never, never
Can pain and rapture
So wild a music,
So sweet a song,
List in the moonlight—
Listen again
O never, never !

O heart still thy beating :
O bird, thy song !
Too deep the rapture
Of this new sorrow.
White falls the moonshine
Here, where we gather'd
The snow-pure blossoms,
The Flowers of Dream :
Here, when the sunlight
On that glad day
Flooded the mosses
With golden wine,
And deep in the forest,

Epilogue

Joy passed us, laughing,
Laughing low,
While ever behind her
Rose lovely, delicate,
Beautiful, beautiful,
The fadeless blossoms,
The Flowers of Dream.
Be still, O beating,
O yearning heart !
Here there is silence . . .
Silence . . . Silence . . .
O beating heart !

Here, in the sunshine,
Together we gather'd
The perfect blooms :
And now in the gloaming,
Here, where the moonlight,
Lies like white foam on
The dark tides of night,
Here is one only,
Longing forever,
Longing, longing
With passion and pain.

Come, O Belovèd !
O heart, be still !
Nay, through the silence
Cometh no answer,

Epilogue

But only, only
The sweet subsiding
Of this wild strain
Now lost in the thickets
Down in the hollows.

Hark . . . rapture outwelling !
O song of joy !
Glad voice of my passion
Singing there
Out of the heart of
The fragrant darkness !
O flowers at my feet,
White beautiful flowers,
That whisper, whisper
My soul's desire !
O never, never
Lost though afar,
My Joy, my Dream

Too deep the rapture
Of this sweet sorrow,
Of this glad pain :
O heart, still thy beating,
O bird, thy song !

POEMS
1889–1893

OCEANUS

I

While still the dusk impends above the
glimmering waste
A tremor comes : wave after wave turns
silvery bright :
A sudden yellow gleam athwart the east is
traced :
The waning stars fade forth, swift perish-
ing pyres.
The moon lies pearly-wan upon the front
of Night.
Then all at once upwells a flood of golden
light
And a myriad waves flash forth a myriad
fires :
Now is the hour the amplest glory of life to
taste,
Outswimming towards the sun upon the
billowy waste.

II

The pure green waves ! with crests of
dazzling foam ashine,
Onward they roll : innumerably grand,
they beat

A wild and jubilant triumph-music all
    divine !
  The sea-fowl, their white kindred of the
    spray-swept air,
  Scream joyous echoes as with wave-
    dipped pinions fleet
  They whirl before the blast or vanish
    'mid blown sleet.
  In loud-resounding, strenuous, conquering
    play they fare,
Like clouds, high over head, forgotten lands
    i' the brine—
Great combing deep-sea waves with sunlit
    foam ashine.

III

On the wide wastes she lives her lawless,
    passionate life :
  Enslaved of none, the imperious mighty
    Sea !
How glorious the music of her waves at strife
  With all the winds of heaven that, fiercely
    wooing, blow !
  On high she ever chants her psalm of
    Victory ;
  Afar her turbulent pæan tells that she is
    free ;
  The tireless albatross with wings like
    foam or snow

Flies leagues on leagues for days, and yet
    the world seems rife
With nought save windy waves and the Sea's
    wild free life !

IV

How oft the strange, wild, haunting glamour
    of the Sea,
    The strange, compelling magic of her
      thrilling Voice,
Have won me, when, 'mid lonely places, wild
    and free
    As any wand'ring wind, I have heard
      along the shore
    The wondrous ever-varying Sea-song loud
      rejoice.
    I have seen a snowy petrel, arising, poise
    Above the green-sloped wave, then pass
      for evermore
From keenest sight, and I have thought that
    I might be
Thus also deathward lured by glamour of the
    Sea.

V

Hark to the long resilient surge o' the
    ebbing tide ;
    With shingly rush and roar it foams adown
      the strand :

The great Sea heaves her restless bosom far
 and wide—
  Heedless she seems of winds and all the
   forceful laws
  That bar her empire over the usurping
   Land :
  Enough, she dreams, is her imperial
   command
  To make the very torrents, waveward
   falling, pause :
She scorns the Bridegroom-Land, yet is a
 subject Bride
For she must come and go with each re-
 current tide.

VI

On moonless nights, when winds are still,
 her stealthy waves
  Creep towards the listening land ; with
   voices soft and low
They whisper strange sea-secrets 'mid the
 hollow caves :
  A wondrous song it is that rises then and
   falls !
  Deep-buried memories of the ancient long-
   ago,
  Confused strange echoes of some vanished
   old world woe,
  Weird prophecies reverberant round those
   wave-worn walls :

When loud the wrathful billows roar and the
      Sea runes
Her deepest mourning broods beneath the
      foaming waves.

VII

As some aerial spirit weaves a rainbow-veil
  Of mist, his high immortal loveliness to
    hide ;
So too thy palpitant waters, duskily pale,
  Oft-times take on a sudden splendour wild.
  Then thy sea-horses rise, fierce prancing
    side by side,
  And—like the host of the dead-arisen—ride
  Ghastly afar to bournes where all the dead
    lie piled ! . . .
Superb, fantastic, crown'd with flying splen-
  dours frail,
Thou, when in dreams, thou weav'st thy
    phosphorescent veil !

VIII

Vast, vast, immeasurably vast, thy dreadful
  peace
  When heaving with slow mighty breath
    thou liest
In utter rest, and dost thy ministering winds
  release

So that with folded wings they too subside,
Floating through hollow spaces, though
    the highest
Stirs his long tremulous pinions when thou
    sighest !
Then in thy soul, that doth in fathomless
    depths abide;
All wild desires and turbulent longings cease—
Profound, immeasurable then, thy dreadful
    peace !

IX

But in thy noon of night, serene as death,
    when under
The terrible silence of that archèd dome
Not a lost whisper ev'n of thy wandering
    thunder
    Ascends like the spiral smoke of perishing
        flame;
    Nor dying wave on thy swart bosom sinks
        in foam—
    Then, then the world is thine, thy heri-
        tage, thy home !
    What then for thee, O Sea, thou Terror !
        or what name
To call thee by, thou Sphinx, thou Mystery,
    thou Wonder—
Above thou art Living Death, Oblivion
    under !

A PARIS NOCTURNE

Over the lonesome hollows
And secret haunts of the river,
Past fields and homestead and village,
Past the grey wharves and the piers
The darkness moves like a veil,
Save when obscure, vast, nigrescent
Flakes from the travelling gloom
Slant westward great fans of blackness.

Then a mist of radiance,
Lamps with red lights and yellow,
Foam-white, and blue as an ice-floe,
Lamps intermingling with gas-light,
Leagues of wind-wavered gas-light,
Lamps on the masts of barges,
Lamps upon sloops and on steamers,
Lamps below quays and dark bridges,
Yellow and red and green,
Like a myriad growths phosphorescent
When a swamp, erewhile flooded with
    waters,

A Paris Nocturne

Lies low to the stare of the moon
And the stealthy white breath of the wind.

And, over all, one light
Palpitant, circular, wide,
Sweeping the city vast—
Yonder, beyond where in shadow
The thronged Champs-Elysées are filling
With echoes of human voices,
With shadows of human lives,
With phantoms of vampyre-vices—
Beyond where the serpentine river
Curves in a coil gigantic,
And straight, a thin shaft, through the
    vagueness
Soars the high lighthouse of Paris,
Soars o'er the sea of the city
With all its shoals and its terrors,
Its perilous straits and its breakers,
High o'er the brightness and splendour
Of shores where the sirens sing ever.

Then, shadows enmassed once again :
And the river moving slowly,
And the hills making darkness deeper.
The lamps now fewer and fewer—
Fewer the red lights and yellow,
Till only a dusky barge
Moves like a water-snake

A *Paris Nocturne*

On the face of a dark lagoon,
A stealthy fire 'mid the stillness ;
While from a weir in the distance
Comes a sound like the cry of waters
When the tides and the sea-winds gather
And the sands of the dunes are scattered
In the scud of the spray.

ROBERT BROWNING

One who never turned his back but marched breast
forward,
Never doubted clouds would break,
Never dreamed, though right were worsted, wrong
would triumph :
Held we fall to rise, are baffled to fight better,
Sleep to wake.

(Died at the Palazzo Rezzonico, Venice, December 12,
1889.)

So, it is well : what need is there to mourn ?
What of the darkness was there, of the
dread,
Of all the pity of old age forlorn
When the swift mind and hand are
though as dead ?
Nothing : the change was his that comes to
days
When, after long, rich, restful afternoons,
A sudden flush of glory fills the skies :
Thereafter is the peace of dream-fraught
moons,
And then, oh ! then for sure, in the eastern
ways
At morn, once more Life's golden floods
arise.

Robert Browning

Ay, it is well : what better fate were his ?
  Why wish for him the twilight-greyness
      drear ?
He hath not known the bitter thing it is
  To halt, and doubt, grope blindly, tremble,
      fear :
The reverend snows above his forehead
    brought
    No ominous hints of that which might not
      be,
      No chill suggestion of the ephemeral soul:
    Unto the very end 'twas his to see
Failure no drear climacteric, but wrought
    To nobler issues, a victorious goal.

There, where the long lagoons by day and
    night
  Feel the swift journeying tides, in ebb and
    flow,
Move inward from the deep with sound and
    light
  And splendour of the seas, or outward go
Resurgent from the city that doth rest
  Upon the flood even as a swan asleep,
    Or as a lily 'mid encircling streams,
    Or as a flower a dusky maid doth keep,
An orient maid, upon her love-warm breast,
    Thrilled with its inspiration through her
      dreams—

There, in the city that he loved so well,
  And with the sea-sound in his ears, the
    sound
Of healing waters in their miracle
  Of changeless and regenerative round,
The strange and solemn silence that is
    death
  Came o'er him. 'Mid the loved ones near
    The deep suspense of the last torturing
      hope
    Hung like a wounded bird, ere swift and
      sheer
It fall with the last frail exhausted breath
    And feeble fluttering wings that cannot
      ope.

There death was his : within his golden
    prime,
  Painless, serene, unvanquished, undis-
    mayed,
He fronted the dark lapse of mortal time
  With eyes alit, through all the gathering
    shade,
With the strange light that clothes immortal
    things—
  Beauty, and Truth, Faith, Hope, and Joy
    and Peace,
    The garnished harvest of our human
      years,

226

Fair dreams and hopes that triumphed o'er
    surcease,
The immaculate sweetness of all bygone
    Springs,
    The rainbow-glory of transfigured tears.

Over him went the Powers, the Dreams, the
    Graces,
The invisible Dominations that we know
Despite the mystic veil that hides their
    faces,
The immortal faces that divinely glow :
Fair Hope was there to take him by the
    hand ;
    White Aspirations smiled about his bed ;
    Desires and Dreams moved gently by
      his side ;
    Beauty stooped low, and shone upon the
      dead ;
Joy spake not, for, from out the Deathless
    land,
    She led God's loveliest gift, his long-lost
      Bride.

Oh, what a trivial mockery then was this,
    The change we so involve with alien
      terror :
How lorn in light of that supernal bliss
    The ruinous wrecking folly of our error !

227

Sweet beyond words the meeting that was
      there,
  Sweet beyond words the deep-set yearning
      gaze,
    Sweet, sweet the voice that long had
      silent been !
Ah, how his soul, beleagured by no maze,
No glooms of Death, i' that Paradisal air
    Knew all was well, since She was there,
      his Queen.

They are not gone, those Dreams, Fair
      Hopes, and Graces,
  Those Powers and Dominations and
      Desires,
They are not passed, though veiled the
      immortal faces,
  Though dimmed meanwhile their eyes'
      wild starry fires.
Meanwhile, it may be, on wan wings and
      slender
  Invisible to mortal gaze, they gleam
    In solemn, sad, processional array
  There where the sunshafts through stained
      windows stream,
And flood the gloomful majesty with
      splendour,
    And charm the aisles from out their
      brooding grey.

They are not gone : nor shall they ever
    vanish,
  Those precious ministers of him, our Poet :
What madness would it be for one to banish,
  To barter his inheritance, forego it,
For some phantasmal gift, some transient
    boon !
    Thus would it be with us were we to turn
      Indifferently aside, when *they* draw
      nigh,
  To look with callous gaze, nor once discern
How swift they come and go, how all too
    soon
    They evade for ever the unheeding eye.

They are not gone : for wheresoe'er there
    liveth
  One hope his song inspired—whom *they*
  inspired—
Yea, wheresoever in one heart there breatheth
An aspiration by his ardour fired :
Where'er through him are souls made serfs
  to Beauty,
  Where'er through him hearts stir with
    lofty aim,
    Where'er through him men thrill with
    high endeavour,
  There shall these ministers breathe low his
    name,

Linked to ideals of Love and Truth and
    Duty,
    And all high things of mind and soul,
    for ever.

No carven stone, no monumental fane;
    Can equal this : that he hath builded deep
A cenotaph beyond the assoiling reign
    Of Her whose eyes are dusk with Night
    and Sleep,
Queenly Oblivion : no Pyramid,
    No vast, gigantic Tomb, no Sepulchre
    Made awful with imag'ries of doom,
Evade her hand who one day shall inter
Man's proudest monuments, as she hath hid
    The immemorial past within her womb.

For he hath built his lasting monument
    Within the hearts and in the minds of men :
The Powers of Life around its base have bent
    The Stream of Memory; our furthest ken
Beholds no reach, no limit to its rise ;
    It hath foundations sure ; it shall not
    pass ;
    The ruin of Time upon it none shall see,
    Till the last wind shall wither the last
    grass;
Nay, while man's Hopes, Fears, Dreams, and
    Agonies
    Uplift his soul to Immortality.

THE MAN AND THE CENTAUR

The Man

Upon the mountain-heights thou goest;
  As swift as some fierce wind-swept flame ;
Thy doom thou scornest while thou knowest
  Men mock thy name.

But thou—thou hast the mountain-splen-
    dour,
  The lonely streams, blue lakes serene,
Wouldst thou these virgin haunts surrender
  For man's demesne ?

Wouldst thou, for peaks where eagles gather,
  Where moon-white skies slow flush with
    dawn;
Where, drenched with dew thy chieftain-
    father
Is far withdrawn—

Wouldst thou all these exchange, give over
  Thy wild free joys and all delights,
Thy proud and passionate mountain-lover,
  Thy starry nights;

The Man and the Centaur

For that drear life in huddled places
　　Where men like ants move to and fro
· Tired men, with ever on their faces
　　The shadow of woe ?

THE CENTAUR

I would not change—did not the waters
ᵇ Did not the winds, all living things
Proclaim that we, the sons and daughters
　　Of Time's first kings,

That we must change and pass and perish
　　Even as autumnal leaves that fall ;
Even as the wind the hill-flowers cherish,
　　At Winter's call :

That we, even we, should know no morrow,
　　For as our body, so our soul :
O human, fair thy life of sorrow,
　　Thou hast a Goal !

DIONYSOS IN INDIA

(Opening Fragment of a Lyrical Drama)

Opening Scene :

Verge of an upland glade among the Himalayas.

Time : Sunrise

FIRST FAUN
. . . Hark ! I hear
Aerial voices—

SECOND FAUN
Whist !

FIRST FAUN
It is the wind
Leaping against the sunrise, on the heights.

SECOND FAUN
No, no, yon mountain-springs—

FIRST FAUN
Hark, hark, oh, hark !—
233

Second Faun

Are budding into foam-flowers : see, they
    fall
Laughing before the dawn—

First Faun

           Oh, the sweet music !

Child-Faun

*(Timidly peeping over a cistus, uncurling
    into blooms.)*

Dear brother, say, oh say, what fills the air ?
The leaves whisper, yet is not any wind :
I am afraid.

First Faun

        Be not afraid, dear child :
There is no gloom.

Child-Faun

        But silence : and—and—then,
The birds have suddenly ceased : and see,
    alow
The gossamer quivers where my startled
    hare—
Slipt from my leash—cow'rs 'mid the fox-
    glove-bells,
His eyes like pansies in a lonely wood !
Oh, I am afraid—afraid—though glad :—

SECOND FAUN

Why glad ?

CHILD-FAUN

I know not.

FIRST FAUN

Never yet an evil god
Forsook the dusk. Lo ! all our vales are
    filled
With light : the darkest shimmers in pale
    blue :
Nought is forlorn : no evil thing goeth by.

SECOND FAUN

They say—

FIRST FAUN
What ? who ?

SECOND FAUN

They of the hills : they say
That a lost god—

FIRST FAUN
Hush, hush : beware !

SECOND FAUN

And why ?
There is no god in the blue empty air ?
Where else ?

First Faun

There is a lifting up of joy :
The morning moves in ecstasy.   Never !
Oh, never fairer morning dawned than this.
Somewhat is nigh !

Second Faun

Maybe : and yet I hear
Nought, save day's familiar sounds, nought
see
But the sweet concourse of familiar things.

First Faun

Speak on, though never a single leaf but
hears,
And, like the hollow shells o' the twisted nuts
That fall in autumn, aye murmuringly holds
The breath of bygone sound.   We know not
when—
To whom—these little wavering tongues
betray
Our heedless words, wild wanderers though
we be.
What say the mountain-lords ?

Second Faun

That a lost god
Fares hither through the dark, ever the dark.

Dionysos in India

FIRST FAUN
What dark ?

SECOND FAUN
    Not the blank hollows of the night :
Blind is he though a god : forgotten graves
The cavernous depths of his oblivious eyes.
His face is as the desert, blanched with ruins.
His voice none ever heard, though whispers
    say
That in the dead of icy winters far
Beyond the utmost peaks we ever clomb
It hath gone forth—a deep, an awful woe.

FIRST FAUN
What seeks he ?

SECOND FAUN
    No one knoweth.

FIRST FAUN
                Yet a god,
And blind !

SECOND FAUN
    Ay so : and I have heard beside
That he is not as other gods ; but from vast
    age—
So vast, that in his youth those hills were wet
With the tossed spume of each returning tide—

He hath lost knowledge of the things that
    are,
All memory of what was, in that dim Past
Which was old time for him ; and knoweth
    nought,
Nought feels, but inextinguishable pain.
Titanic woe and burden of long æons
Of unrequited quest.

FIRST FAUN

              But if he be
Of the Immortal Brotherhood, though blind,
How lost to them ?

SECOND FAUN

         I know not, I. 'Tis said—
Lython the Centaur told me in those days
When he had pity on me in his cave
Far up among the hills—that the lost god
Is curs'd of all his kin, and that his curse
Lies like a cloud about their golden home :
So evermore he goeth to and fro—
The shadow of their glory . . .
                  Ay, he knows
The lost beginnings of the things that are :
We are but morning-dreams to him, and
    Man
But a fantastic shadow of the dawn :
The very Gods seem children to his age,

238

Who reigned before their birth-throes filled
    the sky
With the myriad shattered lights that are the
    stars.

FIRST FAUN

Where reigned this ancient God ?

SECOND FAUN

                 Old Lython said
His kingdom was the Void, where evermore
Silence sits throned upon Oblivion.

FIRST FAUN

What wants he here ?

SECOND FAUN

                 He hateth Helios,
And dogs his steps.   None knoweth more.

FIRST FAUN

                      Aha !
I heed no dotard god !   Behold, behold,
My ears betrayed me not : Oh, hearken now !

CHILD-FAUN

Brother, O brother, all the birds are wild
With song, and through the sun-splashed
    wood there goes
A sound as of a multitude of wings.

239

SECOND FAUN

The sun, the sun ! the flowers in the grass !
Oh, the white glory !

FIRST FAUN
          'Tis the Virgin God !
Hark, hear the hymns that thrill the winds
    of morn,
Wild pæans to the light ! The white
    processionals !
They come ! They come ! . . .

BALLAD OF THE SONG OF THE
SEA-WIND

What is the song the sea-wind sings—
  The old, old song it singeth for aye ?
When abroad it stretches its mighty wings
  And driveth the white clouds far away,—
  What is the song it sings to-day ?
From fire and tumult the white world came,
  When all was a mist of driven spray
And the whirling fragments of a frame !

What is the song the sea-wind sings—
  The old, old song it singeth for aye ?
It seems to breathe a thousand things
  Ere the world grew sad and old and grey—
  Of the dear gods banished far astray—
Of strange wild rumours of joy and shame !
  The Earth is old, so old, To-day—
Blind and halt and weary and lame.

What is the song the sea-wind sings—
  The old, old song it singeth for aye ?
Like a trumpet blast its voice out-rings,
  The world spins down the darksome way !
  It crieth aloud in wild dismay,

Ballad of the Song of the Sea-Wind

The Earth that from fire and tumult came
  Draws swift to her weary end To-day,
Her fires are fusing for that last Flame!

ENVOY

What singeth the sea-wind thus for aye,
  From fire and tumult the white world came!
What is the sea-wind's cry To-day—
  Her central fires make one vast flame!

SONNETS

1893

SONNET-SEQUENCE

I

Where have I known thee, dear, in what
  strange place,
Midst what caprices of our alien fate,
Where have I bowed, worshipping this thy
  face,
And hunger'd for thee, as now, insatiate ?
Tell me, white soul, that through those
  starry veils
Keep'st steadfast vigil o'er my wavering
  spirit,
On what far sea trimm'd we our darkling
  sails
When fell the shadow o'er that we now
  inherit ?
Two tempest-driven souls were we, or glad
With the young joy that recks of no to-
  morrow :
Or were we as now inexplicably sad
Before the coming twilight of new Sorrow ?
Did our flesh quail as now this poor flesh
  quails,
Our faces blanch, as mine, as thine that
  pales !

II

Out of the valley of the Shadow of Death
Who cometh, through the haunted Hollow
 Land ?
On those tired lips of mine whose quickening
 breath,
In this long yearning clasp whose tremulous
 hand ?
O, is it death or dream, madness, or what
Fantastic torture of the chemic brain;
That brings thee here, as thus, when all
 forgot,
Thy body sleeps, as mine doth, free from
 pain ?
What is the brooding word upon thy lips
O beautiful image of my heart's desire ?
What is the ominous shadow of eclipse
That dusks those veilèd eyes' redeeming
 fire ?
O soul whom I from life to life have sought;
What menace haunteth joy so dearly bought ?

III

This menace :—of remembrance that must
    come :
This menace :—of the waking that must be.
O soul, let the rhythm of life itself grow
    dumb
And be the song of death our litany :
Let the world perish as a perishing fire,
For us be less than ashes without flame,
So that we twain our last breath here
    suspire,
Here where none uttereth word, none calleth
    name.
For in the Hollow Land is utter peace,
The magic spell which hath no first or last,
But all that never ceaseth here doth cease
And what would know no death is long
    since past :
Only one thing endures where all expire—
The inviolate rapture of fulfilled desire.

IV

Where art thou, Love !   Lo, I am crucified
Here on the bitter tree of my suspense,
And my soul travails in my quivering side
Wild with the passionate longing to go
 hence.
Where would it voyage, lost, bewildered
 soul
If from the body's warm white home it
 strayed :
Even as the wild-fox would it find its hole,
Even as the fowls of the air would it find
 shade ?
Yea, dear, with winnowing wings there
 would it fly
To fold them on the whiteness of thy breast,
And all its passion breathe into thy sigh,
Fulfil the uttermost peace of perfect rest :
And passing into thee as its last goal
Should know no more this bitter-sweet
 control.

V

Dear, through the silence comes a vibrant
    call,
Thy voice, thy very voice it is, O Sweet !
Yet who shall scale the dread invisible wall
That guards the Eden where our souls
    would meet ?
O veil of flesh, O dull mortality,
Is there no vision for the enfranchised eyes :
Must we stoop low thro' Death's green-
    glooms to see
The immaculate light known of our wingèd
    sighs ?
Nay, Love, of body or soul no shadow or
    gloom
Can always, always, thee and me dispart ;
Soul of my soul, thro' the very gates of
    Doom
Even as deep to deep, heart crieth to
    heart—
Yea, as two moving waves on Life's wild
    sea,
We meet, we merge, we are one, I thou,
    thou me !

VI

" And dost thou love me not a whit the
    less :
And is thy heart as tremulous as of yore,
And do thine eyes mirror the wonderful-
    ness,
And do thy lips retain their magic lore ? "
What, Sweet, can these things be, ev'n in
    thy thought,
And I so briefly gone, so swiftly come ?
Nay, if the pulse of life its beat forgot
This speaking heart would not thereby be
    dumb.
I love thee, love thee so, O beautiful Hell
That dost consume heart, brain, nerves,
    body, soul
That even my immortal birthright I would
    sell
Were Heaven to choose, or Thee, as my one
    goal.
Sweet love fulfilled, they say, the common
    lot !
He who speaks thus, of real love knoweth
    not.

VII

The dull day darkens to its close. The
    sheen
Of a myriad gas-jets lights the squalid night.
There is no joy, it seems, but what hath
    been :
There is nought left but semblance of
    delight.
Nay, is it so ? Down this long darkling
    way
What surety is there for the hungry heart,
What vistas of white peace, rapt holiday
Of the tired soul forlorn, thus kept apart ?
Oh, hearken, hearken, love ! I cannot
    wait :
Drear is the night without, the night within :
I am so tired, so tired, so baffled of our
    fate,
The very sport it seems of our sweet sin :
Oh, open, open now, and bid me stay,
Who almost am too tired, too weak, to
    pray.

VIII

And so, is it so ? the long sweet pain is
    over ?
The dear familiar love must know a change ?
No more am I, no more, to be your lover,
But life be cold once more, and drear, and
    strange.
We have sinned, you say, and sorrow must
    redeem
All the cruel largess of our passionate love,
And we, at the last, content us with a
    dream
Who have known a hell below, a heaven
    above !
Well, be it so : thy life I shall not darken :
Thy dream, for me, shall be disturbed no
    more :
Thine ears, by day or night, shall never
    hearken
The coming of the steps thou lovedst of
    yore :
And if, afar, a lost wild soul blaspheme,
Thou shalt not know it in thy peace supreme.

AN UNTOLD STORY

I

When the dark falls, and as a single star
The orient planets blend in one bright ray
A-quiver through the violet shadows far
Where the rose-red still lingers 'mid the
    grey :

And when the moon, half-cirque around her
    hollow,
Casts on the upland pastures shimmer of
    green :
And the marsh-meteors the frail lightnings
    follow,
And wave lapse into wave with amber
    sheen—

O then my heart is full of thee, who never
From out thy beautiful mysterious eyes
Givest one glance at this my wild endeavour,
Who hast no heed, no heed, of all my sighs :
Is it so well with thee in thy high place
That thou canst mock me thus even to my
    face ?

II

Dull ash-grey frost upon the black-grey fields:
Thick wreaths of tortured smoke above the
    town :
The chill impervious fog no foothold yields,
But onward draws its shroud of yellow
    brown.

No star can pierce the gloom, no moon
    dispart :
And I am lonely here, and scarcely know
What mockery is " death from a broken
    heart,"
What tragic pity in the one word : Woe.

But I am free of thee, at least, yea free !
No more thy bondager 'twixt heaven and
    hell !
No more there numbs, no more there
    shroudeth me
The paralysing horror of thy spell :
No more win'st thou this last frail wor-
    shipping breath,
For twice dead he who dies this second
    death.

THE VEILS OF SILENCE

Three veils of Silence, Summer draws
    apace.
The noon-tide Peace that broods on hill and
    dale,
That passes o'er the sea and leaves no trace,
That sleeps in the moveless clouds' move-
    less trail :

The wave of colour deepening day by day,
The yellow grown to purple on the leas,
Blue within there beyond the dusky ways ;
A green-gloom dusk within the grass-green
    trees.

The third veil no man sees. She weaves it
    where
Beneath the fret and fume tired hearts
    aspire
And long for some divine impossible air.
Out of Man's heart she weaves this veil of
    Rest—
Sweet anodyne for all the feverish quest
And ache of inarticulate Desire.

WRITTEN BY THE SEA

Sweet are white dreams i' the dusk, yet
    sweeter far
When the sea-music fills those haunting
    dreams :
When light survives alone in each white star
And in the far white shine of a myriad
    gleams :
When from white flowers, that through the
    violet gloom
Shine faintly phosphorescent, strange
    breaths steal
And in the lamp-lit silence of the room
The longing, yearning soul makes mute
    appeal :
When nought is heard, and yet the tired
    hands stray
To meet white dream-like hands soft floating
    by :
When the disanchor'd mind sails far away
'Mid the suspense of an imagined sigh—
'Tis thee, 'tis thee, O dear white soul, 'tis
    thee,
White Joy, white Peace, white Balm that
    healeth me !

THE MENACE OF AUTUMN

Amber and yellow and russet, gold and red,
The autumnal leaves dream they are summer
    flowers :
Day after day the windless sunny hours
With feet of flame pass softly overhead :

Day after day over each perishing leaf
The windless hours pass with slow-fading
    flame :
No song is heard where floods of music
    came ;
Long garner'd on the fields the final sheaf.

One day a wild and ravishing wind will rise,
One day a paralysing frost will come,
And all this glory be taken unaware :
Dark branches then will lean against the
    skies,
Sear leaves will drift the forest-pathways
    dumb,
And wold and woodland lie, austere and
    bare.

AFTERMATH

The herald redbreast sings his winter lays,
The fieldfares drift in flocks adown the
    weald :
The turbulent rooks gather on every field,
And clamorous starlings dare our garden-
    ways :

O beautiful garden-ways, not grown less
    dear
Because the rose has gone, and briony waves
Where lily and purple iris have their graves,
Or that, where violets were, the asters rear.

Lo, what a sheen of colour lingers still,
Though the autumnal rains and frost be
    come :
The tall dishevelled sunflowers, stooping,
    spill
Lost rays of sunshine o'er the tangled
    mould,
While everywhere, touched with a glory of
    gold,
Flaunts the imperial chrysanthemum.

FLORA IN JANUARY

The goddess slept.   About her where she lay
Dead pansies, fragrant still, and the myriad
    rose :
Adream 'mid the fallen drift, she woke one
    day,
And the blooms stirred, seeing her eyes
    unclose.

The oaks and beeches stood in disarray,
Gaunt, spectral, dark, in dismal phantom
    rows ;
She smiled, and there was a shimmer 'mid
    the grey
And sudden fall of the first winter-snows.

But when, tired with the icy blossoms of the
    air,
She slept once more, and all the snow was
    over,
She dreamed of Spring and saw his sunlit
    hair,
And heard the whisper of her laughing
    lover :
But while she dreamed, the dead blooms
    had grown fair
And Christmas-roses made a veil above her.

POEMS

1893–1905

FROM OVERSEA

From oversea—
   Violets for memories,
I send to thee ;

Let them bear thoughts of me,
   With pleasant memories
To touch the heart of thee,
   Far oversea.

A little way it is for love to flee,
   Love wing'd with memories,
Hither to thither oversea.

SONG

Love in my heart : oh, heart of me, heart
    of me !
Love is my tyrant, Love is supreme.
What if he passeth, oh, heart of me, heart
    of me !
Love is a phantom, and Life is a dream !

What if he changeth, oh, heart of me, heart
    of me !
Oh, can the waters be void of the wind ?
What if he wendeth afar and apart from me,
    What if he leave me to perish behind ?

What if he passeth, oh, heart of me, heart
    of me !
A flame i' the dusk, a breath of Desire ?
Nay, my sweet Love is the heart and the
    soul of me
    And I am the innermost heart of his
    fire !

Love in my heart : oh, heart of me, heart
    of me !
Love is my tyrant, Love is supreme.
What if he passeth, oh, heart of me, heart
    of me !
    Love is a phantom, and Life is a dream !

THE SUN LORD

Low laughing, blithely scorning—
Beware, beware, of flaming wings,
  Love hunts thee down the morning !

His white feet dip i' the hillside springs,
He mocks thy flying terror !
  The woodland with his laughter rings !

He'll make thee his slave to follow,
Nor shall he forgive thee, maid, thine error,
  Who spied thee hid in the hollow.

Too late, too late the warning !
Behold the flash of flaming wings—
  Love hath thee now i' the morning !

THE SUMMER WOMAN

O wild bee humming in the gorse,
  O wild dove croodling in the woods,
Know ye not she is false as fair,
  A sweet Caprice with bitter moods ?

For bitter-sweet her wild kiss is,
  And bitter-sweet her haunting voice :
How oft my eyes have filled with tears
  When she hath bid me to rejoice !

O loved Caprice, is thine the fault
  Or is the bitterness all mine !
Art thou the quenchless Thirst of Joy
  And I the lees of thy spilt wine ?

Oh, greenness, greenness everywhere,
  Oh, whisper of green leaves, green grass,
Surely the glory is not gone,
  Surely the glory shall not pass ?

I long for some lost magic thing,
  A voice, a gleam, a joy, a pain :
Wild doves, your old-time strain once more,
  Wild bees, wild bees, come back again !

SYCAMORES IN BLOOM

Like flame-wing'd harps the seed blooms lie
   Amid the shadowy sycamores.
The music of each leaflet's sigh
Thrills them continually,
   The small harps of the sycamores.

Small birds innumerable find rest
   And shelter 'midst the sycamores.
Their songs (of love in a warm soft nest)
Are faintly echoed east and west
   By the red harps o' the sycamores.

The dewfall and the starshine make
   Amidst the shadowy sycamores
Sweet delicate strains ; the gold beams
     shake
The leaves at morn, and swift awake
   The small harps of the sycamores.

O sweet Earth's music everywhere,
   Though faint as in the sycamores :
Sweet when buds burst, birds pair ;
Sweet when as thus there wave in the air
   The red harps of the sycamores.

SPRING'S ADVENT

The Spirit of Spring is in the air ;
  The daffodils wave blithe and free
  To the wind's minstrelsy,
    And everywhere
A green rebirth involves each branchlet bare.

Already from the elm-tree boughs
  The jubilant thrush doth cry aloud ;
  From fallow fields new ploughed
    The plovers rouse ;
In hollow boles no more the squirrels
  drowse.

The blackbird calls his thrilling note ;
  And by each field, and copse, and glade
  The leverets race, the rabbits raid ;
    Where gorse-blooms float
The yellow-yite pipes o'er and o'er by rote.

In the blue arch of sky, cloud-swept,
  The unseen larks are singing ;
  The green grass is springing :
    While nature slept,
Leaf-crown'd, bird-haunted Spring hath
  hither leapt.

Spring's Advent

O joy of winds, and birds, and flowers,
    Of growing grass, of budding leaves,
    Of green and sappy sheaves,
        Of rustling showers,
Sunshine, and   plenitude of   marvellous
    hours.

Thrilled Earth beholds her golden prime
    Returned again ; her heart beats swift.
    Low-laughing, as the spring winds lift
        Their songs sublime,
Mocking, she dares the circling Shadow of
    Time.

THE SUMMER WIND

The bugling of the summer wind
  Is sweet upon the hill :
I love to hear its eddies
  The heather-crannies fill.

It plays upon the bracken
  A blithe fanfarronade :
And thro' the moss-cups whistleth
  " The Fairy Raid."

It leaps from birch to rowan,
  And laugheth long and loud,
Then with a spring is vanished,
  And rideth on a cloud !

THE HILL WATER

There is a little brook,
I love it well :
It hath so sweet a sound
That even in dreams my ears could tell
Its music anywhere.
Often I wander there,
And leave my book
Unread upon the ground,
Eager to quell
In the hush'd air
That haunts its flowing forehead fair
All that about my heart hath wound
A trouble of care :
Or, it may be, idly to spell
Its runic music rare
And with its singing soul to share
Its ancient lore profound :
For sweet it is to be the echoing shell
That lists and inly keeps that murmurous
    miracle.
About it all day long
In this June-tide

The Hill Water

There is a myriad song.
From every side
There comes a breath, a hum, a voice :
The hill-wind fans it with a pleasant noise
As of sweet rustling things
That move on unseen wings,
And from the pinewood near
A floating whisper oftentimes I hear,
As when, o'er pastoral meadows wide;
Stealeth the drowsy music of a weir.
The green reeds bend above it,
The soft green grasses stoop and trail
     therein :
The minnows dart and spin :
The purple-gleaming swallows love it :
And, hush, its innermost depth within,
The vague prophetic murmur of the linn.

But not in summer-tide alone
I love to look
Upon this rippling water in my glen :
Most sweet, most dear, my brook,
And most my own,
When the grey mists shroud every ben,
And in its quiet place
The stream doth bare her face;
And lets me pore deep down into her eyes,
Her eyes of shadowy grey,
Wherein from day to day

The Hill Water

My soul is startled with a new surmise,
Or doth some subtler meaning trace
Reflected from unseen invisible skies.

Dear mountain-solitary, dear lonely brook,
Of hillside rains and dews the vagrant
    daughter,
Sweet, sweet, thy music when I bend above
    thee,
When in thy fugitive face I look ;
Yet not the less I love thee,
When, far away, and absent from thee long,
I yearn, my dark hill-water,
I yearn, I strain to hear thy song,
Brown, wandering water,
Dear, murmuring water !

RAINBOW-SHIMMER

To-day upon the hillside
  I saw a golden fairy ;
Her name is Rainbow-Shimmer,
  But for you and me she's Mary.

For Mary is the mother
  Of all sweet souls that be,
From the angels in heaven
  To the best fish in the sea.

And of all sweet souls that are,
  Fairies are the rarest,
And Mary was a star
  Among the fairest.

She had a golden kingcup
  Her little golden head,
For dress she had a daisy white
  Just tipped with red.

She danced upon a clover leaf
  Still ashine with dew
And the blue sky above was not
  As her blue eyes so blue.

274

Rainbow-Shimmer

Her partner was a sunbeam,
  A partner wild and wary,
Whose reel might even tire
  . The patience of a fairy.

Ah, how the two went dancing
  Among the dewy clover ;
I would that you were Mary
  And I your sunbeam lover !

" Stop, Mary, stop," I whispered;
  " Be not so wild and wary,
I know a little lassie
  Who'd dearly love a fairy ! "

But in a twink she vanished,
  The dewshine dance was over !
Ah, her twinkling laughter
  With her sunbeam lover !

But, hush ! Her hiding-place
  Is not so far apart :
I'll tell you where it is, dear,
  It's deep in Mother's heart.

THE YELLOWHAMMER'S SONG

Out on the waste, a little lonely bird, I flit
    and I sing ;
My breast is yellow as sunshine, and light
    as the wind my wing.

The golden gorse me shelters, in the tufted
    grass is my nest,
And *Sweet, sweet, sweet the world*, though
    the wind blow east or west.

The harebells chime their music, the canna
    floats white in the breeze :
But as for me, I flit to and fro and I sing at
    my ease.

When the thyme is dripping with dew, and
    the hill-wind beareth along
The pungent scent of the gale, loudly I sing
    my morning song.

When the sun beats on the gorse, the broom,
    and the budding heather,
I flit from spray to spray, and my song is of
    the golden weather.

The Yellowhammer's Song

When the moor-fowl sink to their rest, and
    the sky is soft rose-red,
I sing of the crescent moon and the single
    star overhead.

Out on the waste, out on the waste, I flit
    all day as I sing,
Sweet, sweet, sweet is the world—dear world—
    how beautiful everything !

Only a little lonely bird that loveth the
    moorland waste,
And little perhaps of the joy of the world
    is that which I taste ;

But out on the wild, free moorlands or the
    gold gorse-boughs I swing,
And *Sweet, sweet, sweet the world ; oh, sweet !*
    ah, sweet ! the song that I sing.

THE SONG OF THE SEA-WIND

King of the winds, O Wind of the Sea,
When thou sweepest abroad thy voice
    crieth;
Crieth the anguish of living souls
As with the wild storm-rapt soughing of the
    oaks.

Breath of the world, O bitter breath;
King of the winds, O Wind of the Sea !

King of the winds, O Wind of the Sea,
Hitherward blow, by our doors, through
    our souls.
Blow, blow, Euroclydon . . . and as dead
    leaves
Whirl seaward vain hopes and perishing
    dreams.

Breath of the world, O bitter breath,
King of the winds, O Wind of the Sea !

King of the winds, O Wind of the Sea,
Uplift us, resurge us out with thy waves,

The Song of the Sea-Wind

Out on thine infinite heaving breast
Where not a wave breaks but is higher than
    hope.

Breath of the world, O bitter breath,
King of the winds, O Wind of the Sea !

King of the winds, O Wind of the Sea,
In the sweep and shadow of mighty wings
Whirl far this Dream that is life, afar
To the Shores of Joy or the Coasts of Night.

Breath of the world, O bitter breath,
King of the winds, O Wind of the Sea !

King of the winds, O Wind of the Sea,
Before thee my heart bows, for it may be
    that God—
Yea, that it is Thee, O God, who passeth by,
Voicing Thy Word to our souls out of
    infinite space—

Eternal Breath, O bitter-sweet Breath,
Lord of all winds, O Wind of the Sea !

SPANISH ROSES

Roses, roses,
Yellow and red ;
A rose for the living,
A rose for the dead !
Who'll sip their dew ?
There are only a few
Of the yellow and red :
Youth sells its roses
Ere youth is sped.

Roses, roses,
All for delight ;
What of the night ?
Hark, the tramp, tramp,
The scabbard's clamp,
The flaring lamp !
Where is the morning dew ?
Ah, only a few
Drank ere the yellow and red
Lay shrivelled, shrivelled,
Over the dead.

Spanish Roses

Roses, roses,
Buy, oh buy.
The years fly;
'Tis the time of roses.
Here are posies
For one and all,
For lovers that sigh
And for lovers that die :
And for Love's pall
And burial !

Roses, roses, roses, buy, buy, oh buy !
Why delay, why delay, roses also die.
Pink and yellow, blood-red, snow-white,
Roses for dayspring, roses for night !

Buy, buy, oh my roses buy !
A kiss for a kiss, and a sigh for a sigh !

THE SEA-BORN VINE

(A Dionysiac Legend)

The sun leapt up the rose-flushed sky
  And yellowed all the sea's pale blue ;
    The Tyrrhene crew
Uprose and hailed the God on high.

But Dionysos made no sign :
  The shipmen hailed their Lord again,
    Acclaimed His reign,
Then stared upon their guest divine.

" The deep shall swallow thee, fair sir :
  The sea-things shall make thee their
      prey—
    The God obey
Or meet swift death ere thou canst stir ! "

" Ere ye arose, my spirit bowed
  To the Great God unrisen then :—
    Take heed, O men,
Your clamour grow not overloud."

The Sea-Born Vine

" A priest of Bacchus thou !   Behold :
　　On sea-wave here could whelm thy God—
　　　　His mystic rod
Would float foam-crown'd 'mid this wave-
　　　　gold.

" *Ai Evoë !*   Thy voice might fill
　　The waste of sea, the waste of sky,
　　　　Yet thou wouldst die,
Thy god supine on some green hill ! "

Ai Evoë !   The cry thrilled wide :
　　The startled rowers shrank—they saw
　　　　With trembling awe
The conscious waters surge aside.

Ai Evoë !   The waves turn green ;
　　In tendril masses twist and twine
　　　　A mighty vine
Uprises and o'erhead doth lean :

Ai Evoë !   The tendrils cling
　　About the shipmen as they swim
　　　　The Bacchic hymn
The waves chant and the wild winds sing.

Evoë !   Dionysos cries,
　　The seamen and the boat no more
　　　　The shingly shore
Shall feel 'neath known or alien skies.

The Sea-Born Vine

Blue dolphins guide the wave-born vine
  To caves near mystic Ind :
    Only the wind
Murmurs for aye the tale divine.

Ye who deride the gods, beware :
  They are with us evermore ; they brook
    No scornful look ;
Their vengeance fills our mortal air.

Yea, of the jealous gods, take heed :
  One day the earth or sea shall ope
    And vanquish hope—
Ai Evoë be vain indeed !

VENILIA

Exspirare rosas, decrescere lilia vidi . . .
CLAUDIAN.

Along the faint shores of the foamless gulf
I see pale lilies droop, wan roses fall,
And Silence stilling the uplifted wave.

And in the movement of the uplifted wave,
And ere the rose fall, or the lily breathe,
Silence becomes a lonely voice, like hers,
Venilia's, who when love was given wings
And far off flight, mourned ceaseless as a
 dove,
Till bitter Circe made her but a voice
Still lingering as a fragrance in dim woods
When on the gay wind swims the yellow
 leaf.

285

ON A NIGHTINGALE IN APRIL

The yellow moon is a dancing phantom
 Down secret ways of the flowing shade ;
And the waveless stream has a murmuring
   whisper
   Where the alders wave.

Not a breath, not a sigh, save the slow
   stream's whisper :
 Only the moon is a dancing blade
That leads a host of the Crescent warriors
   To a phantom raid.

Out of the Lands of Faerie a summons,
 A long, strange cry that thrills through
   the glade :—
The grey-green glooms of the elm are
   stirring,
   Newly afraid.

Last heard, white music, under the olives
 Where once Theocritus sang and played—
Thy Thracian song is the old new wonder
   O moon-white maid !

286

THE DIRGE OF THE REPUBLIC

(In Memoriam.—E. Z.)

In the great days men heard afar the clarions
    of Hope rejoice :
The hearts of men were shaken as reeds by
    the wind of a Voice.
But now the roll of muffled drums drowns
    'mid the last Retreat
The wild fanfare of perishing hopes, the
    tramp of passing feet.

The winds of heaven are banners lost, are
    pennons of dismay ;
The innumerous legion of the sun toils on
    in disarray ;
The moon that carries freight of gold to
    ransom forth the morn
Sails desolate beneath a myriad starry eyes
    of scorn.

Wild rhetoric, yes : but who shall say what
    metaphors of pain
Are fit for the funeral dirge of a Republic
    slain ?

287

The Dirge of the Republic

High hopes, faiths, dreams, great passions,
    aspirations,
Prove but the trodden, useless, bitter dust of
    weary nations !

That which was great is fallen, that which
    was high is low :
The rising star has sunk again, but in a
    blood-red glow :
The hundred thousand souls that died before
    the golden prime.
Did well, for it is well to miss the Ironies of
    Time.

Faith, Honour, Love, the Noble and the
    True,
These lofty words are pawns of an ignoble
    crew :
How better far to light the Torch with
    flames of cheap desire
Than thus to mock the eyes of man with
    stolen fire !

There is no State broad-based enough upon
    the People's heart
That some day may not hunted be by the
    People's dart :

The Dirge of the Republic

The rebel nerves, the rebel lusts, the rebel
    hounds of life—
If these be loosened from the whip they
    turn to fratricidal strife.

Is this the end of all high dreams above
    thrones trampled under ?
Is this the tinsel chorus left after the noble
    thunder ?
'Twere better, then, than thus to live, thus
    forfeit high renown,
To be true men, and free, " beneath the
    shadow of a Crown " !

INTO THE SILENCE

(*A Death in the West Highlands*)

Ungather'd lie the peats upon the moss ;
  No more is heard the shaggy pony's hoof ;
  The thin smoke curls no more above the
    roof ;
Unused the brown-sailed boat doth idly
  toss
At anchor in the Kyle ; and all across
  The strath the collie scours without
    reproof ;
  The gather'd sheep stand wonderingly
    aloof ;
And everywhere there is a sense of loss.
" Has Sheumais left for over sea ? Nay,
  sir,
  A se'nnight since a gloom came over him ;
  He sicken'd, and his gaze grew vague and
    dim ;
Three days ago we found he did not stir.
He has gone into the Silence. 'Neath yon
  fir
  He lies, and waits the Lord in darkness
    grim."

THE HILL-ROAD TO ARDMORE

There's the hill-road to Ardmore, Mary,
   Here's the glen-road to Ardstrae :
Your home is younder, Mary,
   And mine lies this way.

Will you come by the glen, Mary,
   Or go the hill-road to Ardmore ?
It is now and as you will, Mary,
   For I will ask no more.

'Tis but a score years, Mary,
   Since I bade you to Ardstrae ;
And now you are not there, Mary
   Nor walk the hill-side way.

Is it only a score years, Mary,
   Since we parted by the shore,
And I watched you go, Mary,
   By the hill-road to Ardmore ?

WHITE ROSE

Far in the inland valleys
  The Spring her secret tells ;
The roses lift on the bushes,
  The lilies shake their bells.

To a lily of the valley
  A white rose leans from above :
" Little white flower o' the valley,
  Come up and be my love."

To the lily of the valley
  A speedwell whispers, " No !
Where the roses live are thorns;
  'Tis safe below."

The lily clomb to the rose-bush,
  A thorn in her side :
The white rose has wedded a red rose,
  And the lily died.

ECHOES OF JOY

Only a song of joy
  Wind-blown over the heather,
Somewhere two little hearts
  Thrill and throb together.

Ah, far 'mid the nethermost spheres
  Life and Death live together ;
And deep is their love, without tears,
For they laugh at the shadows of years—
And yet there rings in my ears
    Only a song of joy
  Wind-blown over the heather.

WHEN THE GREENNESS IS COME
AGAIN

The west wind lifts the plumes of the fir,
  The west wind swings on the pine ;
In the sun-and-shadow the cushats stir ;
  For the breath of Spring is a wine
      That fills the wood,
      That thrills the blood,
  When the glad March sun doth shine,
      Once more,
  When the glad March sun doth shine.

When the strong May sun is a song, a song,
  A song in the good green world,
Then the little green leaves wax long
  And the little fern-fronds are uncurl'd ;
  The banners of green are all unfurl'd,
And the wind goes marching along, along,
The wind goes marching along
  The good green world.

IT HAPPENED IN MAY

A maid forsaken
  A white prayer offered
Under the snow of the apple-blossom :
  To whom was it proffered ?
By whom was it taken ?
    Well, I suppose
    Nobody knows.

But somehow, the snows
Of the apple-blossom
  Were changed one day.
A kiss was offered,
    A kiss was taken :
  And lo ! when the maiden looked shyly
    away,
    Of bloom of the apple the boughs were
    forsaken !
But whiter and sweeter grew orange-
    blossom !
    Now this is quite true, I say,
    And it happened in May.

NIGHTINGALE LANE

Down through the thicket, out of the
      hedges,
  A ripple of music singeth a tune . . .
     Like water that falls
     From mossy ledges
With a soft low croon :
       Soon
     It will cease !
No, it falls but to rise—but to rise—but
     to rise !
It is over the thickets, it leaps in the trees,
  It swims like a star in the purple-black
     skies !
     Ah, once again,
     With its rapture and pain,
The nightingale singeth under the moon !

BLOSSOM OF SNOW

" Sing a song of blossom,"
Said little Marjory Brown :
" Why won't it come down,
Here in the town,
  Please ? "
Said little Marjory Brown.

  " Please,
Wind, blow just a breath, for me
  To see
The great white apple-blossoms blow
Just like snow—
Just like snow in our garden before we
 Came back to town,"
 Said little Marjory Brown.

All day and all night
 A wind did blow,
  Marjory laughed at the flying snow
  And its whirling riot :
But at dawn she grew wan and white,
  And was quiet.
And the doctor said,
With his hand on a bowed sobbing head,
" Too late you came up to town
 With little Marjory Brown."

THE DANDELION

A thousand poets have sung the Rose,
  The daisy white, the heather,
  The green grass we lie on
    In summer weather . . .
Of almost every flower that grows,
  But never of the Dandelion,
That the winds of Spring have scattered
    hither and thither !

Is there any more fair to see
  Than this bright fellow
    Who, also, " takes the winds of March
      with beauty " ?
  True his coat in a vulgar yellow,
    And his is a very humble duty . . .
      Merely to be
As joyous as a wave on the sea,
A wave dancing on the great sea,—
Merely to be bright, sunshiny, glad, strong,
    and free,
    As free as a beggar, as proud as a king !

298

The Dandelion

And so, quite as good as the Rose,
  The daisy white, the heather,
    The green grass we lie on
    In summer weather,
Is that flame of the feet of Spring,
  The Dandelion !

THE DREAM-WIND

(Written for Music)

When, like a sleeping child
　　Or a bird in the nest,
The day is gathered
　　To the earth's breast . . .
Hush ! . . . 'tis the Dream-Wind,
　　　Breathing peace,
　　　Breathing rest,
　　Out of the Gardens of Sleep in the West.

Oh, come to me, wandering
　　Wind of the West !
Grey doves of slumber
　　Come hither to rest ! . . .
Hush ! . . . now the wings cease
　　　Below the dim trees . . .
　　And the White Rose of Rest
　　Breathes low in the Gardens of Sleep in the
　　　　West.

TRIAD

From the Silence of Time, Time's Silence
    borrow.
In the heart of To-day is the word of To-
    morrow.
The Builders of Joy are the Children of
    Sorrow.

IN MEMORIAM

He laughed at Life's Sunset Gates
  With vanishing breath :
Glad soul, who went with the Sun
  To the Sunrise of Death.

PERSEPHONEIA

A FRAGMENT

1903

PROLOGUE

*An ancient solitary temple of Persephoneia by
the sea. A dull sunset, burning slowly
over Hybla. Melkos, an old blind priest,
attended by a boy. A brazen glow rests
on Etna, whence issues a thin column of
dusky smoke filled at times with a tongue
of red flame.*

MELKOS

The old dull whisper of the unceasing wave.
[*Sighing.*] The slow sound of the unceasing
    wave.

           [*Displaces a stone with his foot.*

Out of these shadowy hollows of the ocean
Troop the grey dreams that plague the
    minds of men.
Far off Hadranos hears : Enkelados
Puts forth his hands and shapes the sound
    to thought :
And on her lonely Mount where the sunset
    burns
Hybla remoulds in pale invisible flame.

          [*The boy idly plays a note or two.*

Persephoneia

I am too old to fear these Holy Ones،
Hybla Beneficent, why should one fear
The Twilight Goddess, born where the
    Evening star
Hangs o'er the abyss where swims the
    unrisen moon.
Hadrânos loves us not, but hates us not :
Though dreadful to men's ears the baying
    of the hounds
That night and day, a thousandfold,
    engird
His sacred temple with a surge of sound.
Rather the man I fear, the Titan-slave,
Who hates the sovran powers who hold him
    thrall,
And hugs a secret that no god doth know,
Save only her, Demeter, when the frenzy
Terribly moves her calm to dreadful storm—
And him, Poseidon, when in his shell-strewn
    sleep
Deep in the dim green silences he moans
Remembering . .ְ. him rather do I fear,
Enkelados, the Helot of the Gods.
      [*The boy half raises himself, looks
      toward the ancient temple.*

Melkos

Why do you stir, Neanthes ?   Does the light
From off Hyblæan hill draw near the roof ?

Persephoneia

NEANTHES

The she-goat browsing 'mid the yellow
  spurge
Yonder, where the lava crouches like a
  lizard
Nailed to a thorn, looked suddenly up and
  whinnied,
Her ears swung like figs in the wind, and her
  knees
Bent, and she shrank shivering to the
  ground.
  *[He sinks again, and plays a few notes
  on his reed pipe.*

MELKOS

That slow sound of the unceasing wave.
  For ages
These watery fangs have gnawed and torn
  the shore.
  [Again displaces a stone with his foot.
When I was young I sailed three days and
  nights,
Southward three days when the great God
  drowned in fire,
Southward three nights when lost amid pale
  stars
The half-moon waned, and never land I saw,
Nor living thing, save a shadow in the
  calms

Where overhead a white-winged sea-hawk
    flew.
And on the morrow of the fourth I heard
The stifled laughters of a hidden folk,
Hoarse murmurings, a dull tumultuous haste,
With sad sea-voices full of lamentation,
And a single voice that knew not any peace.

NEANTHES

        [Listlessly, without looking up.
Who were these creatures of the salt south
    sea ?

MELKOS

Out of the depths they came, I know not
    whence,
Or what. Poseidon's offspring, they, who
    made
A green and dreadful rumour through the
    wave.

NEANTHES

           [Singing.

Fair is the falling wave, and fair
The paven green sea-halls,
And one who sleepeth sound is sleeping there.

MELKOS

And as in some old dream that swims un-
    sought
Into the unwilling mind, I know once more

Persephoneia

The old fear I felt, and all the horror of
    fear,
When out of the foam and the seas and the
    wind
I heard a voice of vengeance and of wrath
And heard Poseidon calling on the shade
Of that most sacred, dread, and nameless
    god
Who lives below the root of ancient slime
Left by forgotten seas and the most deepset
    fires
Enkelados hath watched, Hadranos seen,
Leaning o'er midnight chasms fill'd witl
    flame.
Loudly he called, and billow on billow leapt ;
Louder, and seas rose, and fell upon seas ;
Loudlier, till the shaken watery domes
That moved as a falling city on Etna moves,
Crag-slipt to gulfs of fathomless abyss,
I saw far-off steadfast stars involved,
Spun round like dust about a chariot wheel.
And all the anguish of his cry was filled
With one name only—hers, whom he begat
A thousand thousand years ago, on her
The stern implacable guardian of mankind
Demeter-Erinnys, on whose name be peace.
That name alone I heard. . . Persephoneia.
    [NEANTHES *again raises himself, looking
    towards the ancient temple.*

Persephoneia

MELKOS

Does the light fall from off the Hyblæan
   hill, Neanthes ?

NEANTHES

Three sea-birds dripping from the foam
Wheeled inland, yonder where the spotted
   snake
Has made her lair under the asphodels,
And one by one withered in fright, and flung
Heavily downward, and all three lie dead.

MELKOS

    [Again to himself, unheeding the boy.
And when like a snowflake blindly up-
   whirled and borne
My frail boat sung from one gulf to another,
And I lay breathless, dead, as one long dead,
Blind, deaf, dumb, senseless, without hope
   or fear,
Who ploughed the furrow of my flying keel ?
That thing I do not know, nor how I escaped
A peril more dire than that which waits for
   ships
For Cumæ bound when Zankle sinks behind.
But on one desolate morrow my grey lips
Knew rain, and all my weary flesh was healed
With warmth and peace, at the coming of a
   calm

Persephoneia

Leaning from heaven on the lapping waters,
And from the violet hollows heavenward
  risen.
And that day, in the hush of afternoon,
I heard a shoreward sighing of the sea
And in my nostrils was the blessed smell
Of grass and earth and trees : so lifting me,
And having made my prayer of thankfulness
To him, the lord Poseidon of the Deep,
I looked . . . and saw a melancholy shore,
A long low lifeless melancholy shore,
Wherefrom, an infinite way, the world
  uprose,
Leaning gigantic . . . the vast womb of her,
The Mother Mountain, and, purpling in the
  west,
Hybla I saw, the Holy Hill : and else,
No single home wherefrom the blue smoke
  toiled.
But this I saw with dread, that ancient
  homes
Hearthless and faded stood among grey
  trees,
And a gaunt bridge hung broken o'er the bed
Of a great river where no water ran,
And old-time gardens all unwall'd, un-
  kempt,
Were green with noisome growth, and fruit-
  less, drear.

Persephoneia

Some fallen columns lay upon the sand
Whereon the lizards fled, and in one place
I saw the image of an unknown God
Within whose cavernous ruin the adder
    curled.
Near by, erect, unshaken, stood a fane
Even that by which this solitary eve
I stand in these my blind and listless years—
Fearing so little, with so little hope,
Yet dimly seeing in the far-off law
The shaping of divine perfected things.
Most drear and solitary it rose thereby,
The columns held the vast grey slab of roof
That still they hold, in whose wind-haunted
    places
The sea-crows built, with melancholy cries
Lifting black wings at sundown and at dawn.
But on that dayset, from the midmost rose
A thin and wavering column of spiced smoke
Such as from altars rise, fragrant with gums,
With wine and frankincense, where gods are
    known ;
And even as I watched, the purple bloom
That Hybla wore, as a priestess wears a robe,
So that the woman and the robe are one,
Took fire : or rather, far below, a sea of
    flame
Swung from its ebb, and with a mighty sigh
From dim abysms reached a fiery crest,

Persephoneia

The conflagration of whose soundless life
Changed Hybla to a molten brazen mass.
Therefrom a concentrated stream of light
Poured near the desolate fane ; but as the
    God
Sank sighing to the underworld his hand
Lingered a brief while here : and the pale
    smoke
Spired suddenly like the crimson breath of
    roses.
      [*The boy again raises himself, looking
        towards the ancient temple.*
Does the light fall from off the Hyblæan
    hill, Neanthes ?

NEANTHES

          A little breath of smoke
Rose from the broken terrace near the
    fane,
No more than from the white ox idly
    breathes
When with wet lips he tastes the morning
    grass.

MELKOS

And then ?

NEANTHES

       A sudden noisy whirl of sparrows
Scattered like leaves around the seaward
    columns :

313

And even as I looked, like leaves they
 fluttered,
Falling and fallen, and now strewn deep they
 lie.

MELKOS

 [Turning his face seaward again.
And even as the curling breath of roses
Wavered again to pale aerial smoke,
Even in that moment I beheld a woman
Standing in silence on the ruin'd terrace
That downward reaches to the lifting wave
Oozy with slimy frondage of the sea.
So tall she was, so noble of mien, so great
In the perfected beauty of repose,
That for a moment all my thoughts beheld
A flawless statue simulating life.
Most pale, most terrible her awful face.
The dark hair lay adown it in great clusters,
Like to the wild vine on the ashy cliff
That on Ætnean Inessa bears the grape
Wherefrom the grey priests of Demeter brew
A fatal juice. The sadness of the hills
Crowned the sheer lonely height that was
 her forehead.
The immemorial whisper of the sea‿
Inhabited the silence of her face :
And in the flamelit darkness of her˙eyes
The melancholy of forgotten things
Was like a rainy dusk in the inlands drear.

314

Persephoneia

In stillness she stood there, immovable,
As Twilight stands in the passes of the hills
When the Noon lifts her blazing wing and
 sheers
Behind the incurring, blank, precipitous
 walls.
Then well I knew a goddess I beheld.

A Voice

O bitter and terrible love of the wave for
 the wind,
 Of the north for the flame,
And the love and the joy and the glory half
 left behind
 For the mockery of a name.

Melkos

What words were these : what bitter song
 from the sea,
Out of the hills, or lifted from the slain ?

Neanthes

Only the wind I heard, and a sigh from the
 sea.
It is gone now, and the far-off sea is still.

Melkos

   [Again turning his face to the sea.
Then I knew a goddess I beheld.

                    [A pause.

315

But sad she was, more sad than I had
    dreamed
The high immortal ones could ever be.
And while I looked I saw that in one hand
A cluster of flowers she held, anemones
Wine-dark in hue, the sunbright celandine
And poppies heavy in a downward flame,
With pale green blossoms of the yellow
    spurge.
But even as I looked a withering came
Like a grey bloom upon them, and that
    bloom
Dusked into ash, and in grey ash they fell
Making an eddy of dust before her feet.
Then a wild dove with sudden clamorous
    wing
Batted the still air of the dreadful peace ;
Circling about her, come I know not whence ;
But even as I looked the grey wing sank
And as a falling dust the cushat fell.
                        [A pause.
Then all my soul rose up in me, and knew
Persephoneia.   *[A pause.*
        And at that dreadful name,
Born on my lips as dawn on a moving wave,
The dark gulfs of her dreadful beautiful
    eyes
Turned slowly upon mine, wherefrom the
    light,

Ebbed, as the withdrawing gleam ebbs from
    a pool
On sundown sands when the seas grow
    suddenly pale.
From that day unto this I have not seen
Goddess nor mortal, maid nor mortal man :
No, nor the grey stairs of Poseidon's home,
Nor Helios lighting torches on the hills,
Nor any queen hour laughing on the slopes
Where the watercourses are, nor almond
    blossom
Foaming the pools where purple iris grow.
No, never once have I beheld my kind ;
Never the goatherd fluting to his flock
Black-feeted kids amid the lava blocks
Stained with old lichen, yellow with flower-
    ing spurge ;
Nor the white train of sacred maids down-
    wending
By the fig-bordered ways of holy Inessa,
Nor the gold filleted ancient men who bow
At Hybla, nor the blue-robed youths who
    stand
Watching the thousand hounds of Hadranon.
Yea, all these weary years I have not seen.
In gracious places I have never heard
The chorus rave, nor the solitary hymn
Peal from the heights of Enna when the
    doves

Gather like flames before the Koré's fane :
Nor laughter in the nightingale-haunted
    woods
When the moon lifts the silver from the
    pools
And ripples it lightly through the rippling
    boughs ;
Never for me the chariot-race, the games,
The sounds of down-falling cars in gladsome
    havens,
The kiss of wife or child, the choric song
Of kings and wars and mighty kings of old,
The bubble from the wine-skin, the gay jibe
And all familiar things of the old-time day,
For I am old and blind : for years on years,
How many years I know not, have been
    blind.
That sorrow came to me because I saw
Divinity unveiled, and for a moment knew
The terrible life of immortality.
The high gods rule us hardly.   If we fail
To seek them in their shrines and holy places
Sorrows are laid on us, and many plagues,
And the awful weight of the superhuman
    frown.
And, if unseen we come upon these folk,
Star-tramplers, sea-shod, kindred of the
    powers
That are the Eternal balance of the world,

Persephoneia

Pitiless are they, or full of dreadful scorn,
Or mockery worse than flushing of the levin.
But I have served her faithfully ; Aweful
    One. . . .
Yea, all these years in blindness and in pain,
In sorrow, loneliness and grievous days
I have not strayed an hour long from her
    shrine.
Few men come here, to this deserted land :
These haste away, so dreadful is the air
Of deathless immemorial decays,
Cities that were, dis-peopled villages,
Gardens, with barren founts and fruitless
    trees,
Old roadways gathered to the prickly-pear,
Dry watercourses where the lizards run
With withered tongues seeking forbidden dew,
And this gaunt solitary ruined fane
Whereon is Silence, terrible and alone.
Yea, I have kept the sacred fire alit
From dusk till dawn, and quenched it at the
    dawn,
And every noon have gathered up the ashes
And thrown them in the grey receding wave.
Yet never has the goddess deigned to me . . .
No, not a word, no, not a little word,
Nor even guerdon given, albeit ease
Or dreamless sleep, or food, or shade, or
    warmth,

Persephoneia

The visitation of unblended hours,
The gifts of song, of prophecy, of dream.
But, when I die, the crow will pick mine eyes,
And if the crawling wave discrown my tomb
The clammy fins of fish will touch my bones.
                [Raising his arms in supplication.
O thou who in thy unknown secret power
Descendeth hither, coming as a wind
That eddies in the grass, and as an eddy
Returning when it wills, in a secret way,
O thou, Persephoneia, whom men worship
High in the holy fane of the sacred Koré
Where Enna rears her consecrated steep
In frowning flanks of basalt from the wilds
Hearken, have pity, give at least a sign. . . .
For I have served thee well, who am broken,
    and blind,
And now am old, and soon shall know no more,
But be a thing that was not, unrecalled.
        [The boy suddenly gives three sharp
          calls on his reed.

MELKOS

Neanthes . . . what ?

NEANTHES

              A shadow suddenly falls
Which nothing casts, where no one is ! . . .
    yonder

Betwixt the columns where the sea gleams
  red,
As a pomegranate on a dark blue leaf.

MELKOS
Quick, boy ! . . . Neanthes . . . does the
  beam of light
From off the Hyblæan hill yet reach the
  roof ?
>   [*Neanthes, leaping to his feet, covers his
>   face, and turns and bounds swiftly
>   away.*

NEANTHES
It comes ! It comes !

MELKOS
>   [*Slowly advancing.*
Hail to the Koré of Enna, hail !
>   [*A pause.*
Persephoneia ! Mother of Life and Death !
  Hail !
Hail, Unbegotten but by the dreams of the
  gods
Foreshaped by him, Poseidon-Hippios,
Foreknown of her, Demeter, the veiled
  Queen !
Hail to the Koré ! Hail, Persephoneia !
>   [*A pause.*

Persephoneia

Though many days have sunk and dark
    nights risen,
Yea, many moons have waxt and waned in
    vain,
And thou hast not revisited this place,
Yet art thou come again, O Holy One !
I know well by the portents, and the awe
That lies on all this breath-suspended shore.
                      [*A pause.*
A sign, a sign, O thou whom I have served
In silent adoration all these years !

A Voice

Go down to the dim waves and bathe thine
    eyes.
Maybe other gods may serve thee there :
Or sleep, or dream. I knew not thou wert
    blind,
Who have never known nor seen that
    worshipper
Save as a shadow flickering in the silence.
Go up to the hill-encircled mountain fane
That frowns on Enna, and then lay thee
    down
On the altar-step, that so, perchance, my
    foot
May for less than a moment burn thy lips.
Then may thy blindness quicken . . . or
    the dark

Persephoneia

Drown in upon thee with a deeper night.
But trouble me no more with faithful
    service,
That, or unfaithful. Here I dwell alone.
      [MELKOS *stands in silence, then slowly*
          moves towards the sea. As in a
          dream he walks slowly, through
          lentisk and tamarisk, often look-
          ing back, half in dread, half in
          expectation.

BALLANTYNE & COMPANY LTD
TAVISTOCK STREET COVENT GARDEN
LONDON